CH00949667

A Survey of Whirlow Hall Containing 189 Acres, 2 Rood, 29 Perches, taken in the year 1720.

Sheffield City Libraries. Hollis Collection. LD 1430.

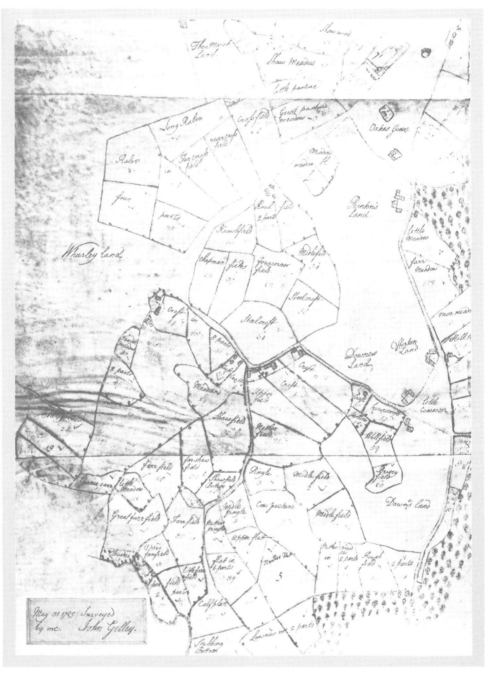

Sheffield City Libraries. Wentworth Woodhouse Muniments Add. Map 18 (part)

WHIRLOW

Old Drinking Trough. Alms Hill near Sheffield. Painted by W. H. Mander, circa 1894.

WHIRLOW

The story of an ancient
Sheffield hamlet

by

SHIRLEY FROST

A first edition limited to 1,000 copies
of which 200 are in hard-back
Reprinted 2004

© SHIRLEY FROST FRGS 1990

Printed by J. W. Northend Ltd.
Sheffield

ISBN 0 901100 25 0 (hard-back)
ISBN 0 901100 26 9 (soft-back)

Front Cover: *The old mellow buildings of Whirlow Hall Farm.*

End Papers: *These historical and intriguing old maps were compiled within five years of one another. The originals of these rare and precious documents, fragile with age, are held in the Sheffield Archives of Sheffield City Libraries. The left hand map is a survey of Whirlow Hall (note the spelling) taken in 1720. It shows the Hall and marks the fields with their names and was possibly updated after the estate was purchased by Thomas Hollis and given to the Hollis Trust in 1726. The right hand page shows the Whirlow section of the map of Ecclesall, surveyed by John Gelley for Mr. John Bright in 1725. In this delightful pictorial map he has not only drawn in the lanes, the fields and their names, but the woods and houses as well.*

Preface

IN 1977 my son Richard and I, intrigued by the old lanes and stone buildings in Whirlow, decided to delve into their history. I am most grateful for all the help he gave me in those early days. I am also grateful to Dr. David Hey, Reader in Local History at Sheffield University, whose lectures I attended and who fuelled my enthusiasm even more.

So many people have helped me with this book as you will see from the long list of acknowledgements. Mr. Joshua Needham and Mr. John Hulley whose families have lived in Whirlow and Ecclesall for generations have shared their considerable knowledge of the area with me. Much of the information is from old documents which are sometimes difficult to read, so although I have tried to cross check as much as possible, please accept my apologies if errors have been made.

Many of the costs and prices quoted are from the days before decimal currency came into use in February 1971, when our money seemed to go so much further. There were twelve pennies in a shilling, twenty shillings in a pound. One shilling was the equivalent of five new pence, which was also the daily rate for men working in Ecclesall Woods in 1730, a sum now difficult to comprehend.

I should like to stress that most of the old buildings mentioned in the text are private property and are not accessible to the general public.

It has been great fun researching the book, the search has been a long and fascinating one and there is still much to discover of Whirlow's long history. I hope you will enjoy reading it as much as I have enjoyed writing it.

ACKNOWLEDGEMENTS

I should like to thank the archivists and staff of the Sheffield Archives and the librarians and staff of the Local Studies Library, Sheffield City Library for their patience and assistance during my research. Also the Director of Libraries and Information Services, Sheffield City Libraries; Olive, Countess Fitzwilliam's Wentworth Settlement Trustees (Wentworth Woodhouse Muniments); the Borthwick Institute of Historical Research; the West Yorkshire Archive Service and the Hollis Trust for permission to quote from their archives. I am indebted to the Ordnance Survey for permission to reproduce the 1854 O.S. Map.

I am grateful to the City Engineer's Department of Sheffield City Council for providing some of the photographs of old buildings in the Whirlow area and to the Sheffield Postcard Company and Sheffield City Library for permission to reproduce photographs and sketches from their collections.

May I thank Mr. Tom Dakin for his helpful advice and expertise, Mrs. Janet Kelly for her good humour in deciphering and typing manuscript and all the people who have helped me with their local knowledge and loan of their precious photographs, including:

The late Mrs. Margaret Bentley
Mrs. David Booker
Mrs. Freda Bradbury
British Steel p.l.c.
Mr. and Mrs. Michael Carter
Mrs. Mary Colver
The Company of Cutlers in Hallamshire
Eadon, Lockwood & Riddle
Mrs. Mary Furness
G.A. Property Services, Saxtons
Mrs. Muriel Greatorex
The late Mrs. Molly Grayson
Mr. and Mrs. Bob Grayson
Greenstreet Photographics Ltd.
Haybrook Property Services
Mr. Horace Mottram
The late Mr. Hubert Nicholson
Lt. Col. Hugh Neill
Miss M. Pearce, Sheffield City Museum
Mr. and Mrs. Paul Proctor
Project 83, Photographic
The late Lady Renwick
Sheffield City Council Department of Land and Planning
Sheffield City Council Department of Design and Buildings Services,
    Highways and Traffic Division
Mr. Donald Shipman
The late Mrs. Shipman
Mr. E. O. Skinner
Mr. Rowland Walker

Finally I should like to thank my family and especially my husband, without whose help and support this book would not have been published.

SHIRLEY FROST 1990

Contents

Subscribers

Fearnehough (Bakewell) Limited

Mr. and Mrs. R. A. Frost

Mr. and Mrs. J. R. Gledhill

Greenstreet Photographics Limited

Hawsons

A. E. Jameson & Co.

Mr. and Mrs. M. P. W. Lee

T. G. Lilleyman & Son Limited

Mr. and Mrs. P. D. Mills

National Westminster Bank PLC

J. W. Northend Limited

P.A. Jewellery Limited

Pinelog Products Limited

H. Ponsford Limited

Mr. and Mrs. P. H. Proctor

Wake Smith & Company

Mr. and Mrs. R. Walker

Mr. and Mrs. R. P. Wilkinson

CHAPTER ONE

Introduction

TUMBLING down from the high moors above Ringinglow a small stream, the Limb Brook, flows through Ecclesall Woods to join the River Sheaf at Abbeydale. This seemingly unimportant brook once separated the ancient kingdoms of Mercia and Northumbria, marking not only the county boundaries of Yorkshire and Derbyshire, but also the ecclesiastical boundaries of Canterbury and York and the parishes of Ecclesall and Dore. It is here between the high moorland and Ecclesall Woods that Whirlow is situated. Part of the Parish of Ecclesall and at one time of the larger Manor of Hallamshire, Whirlow was one of the many hamlets which together made up the Manor of Ecclesall but which are now mainly suburbs of the City of Sheffield. Today Whirlow encompasses the area from Parkhead in the north to Whirlow Bridge in the south and from Broad Elms Lane in the west to Whirlow Park Road in the east.

Whirlow is said to mean a boundary mound and placed as it is on so many boundaries, it is an apt name. Low often refers to a barrow or burial mound. S. O. Addy writing in 1888 felt this applied to Whirlow. At the top of the hill behind Whirlow Hall, overlooking Castle Dyke, is a field which in former times was called the Cocked Hat Field. Ancient field names sometimes point to surnames, crops or physical features which may have disappeared.

The Old Buildings of Whirlow Hall Farm 1990.

1

Cocked Hat Fields in other areas have usually denoted barrows. There was a Cocked Hat Lane at Crookes where two burial urns were found in April 1887. No documented burial remains have been found at Whirlow, it is just supposition, but nevertheless it is an ancient place and it is evident that men were here long before documentary evidence was there to prove it. The Roman road at Stanedge is not far across the moor, there are traces of old English and Norse names and King Ecgbert of Wessex led his army to Dore in AD 829. One of the earliest documents is of a grant of 1341 which mentions John de Horlowe — John of Whirlow. The hamlet had many forms of spelling from Horlow, Hurlowe, Horlowe and Horloo to the more modern versions of Whirlowe, Whirlawe, Whirley and today Whirlow.

The majority of the farm houses and cottages that remain in Whirlow today were built at the end of the 18th Century and mainly at the beginning of the 19th Century. During the centuries that people have been living here, the cottages and farms must have been rebuilt or extended many times. Except in a few instances the farming tenants of Earl Fitzwilliam, the main landlord, were given either partial or total monetary help.

The original cottages were no doubt simple timber framed buildings, possibly cruck-built. The crucks were pairs of large curved timbers standing on stone footings to prevent rot, extended to the roof where they were joined by tie and collar beams. The walls would be of wattle and daub, plastered inside and out to give protection from the weather. By the 17th Century, the walls would be infilled with stone. In Hallamshire there is evidence of many cruck-built buildings and the barns at the Low Farm at Whirlow Hall are a marvellous example.

The end of the Civil War in England saw an upsurge of building and Whirlow was no exception; with the increasing demand for timber, homes were rebuilt in stone. There was a plentiful supply near at hand; the quarries at Brincliffe Edge had been producing fine stone as far back as 1575 and in the 17th Century stone was quarried at Whirlow Lane and Alms Hill; timber was available from Ecclesall Woods.

In 1679-80 considerable alterations were carried out for Sir John Bright, the landlord, on several of the Whirlow farms. These were mostly tenanted by farmers with some standing in the neighbourhood who were probably feeling the need for more comfort. There is every indication that certain farms were only single storey for there is mention of new staircases. Outshots, possibly service rooms, were added to some of the farms, ground floors were paved with stone slabs and new glazing was provided for the windows.

New houses were often built adjacent to the old; around 1686 Robert and Richard Offerton erected a new house at Thrift House, the old house becoming a barn. Thrift House was again rebuilt in 1840. When it was enlarged in 1883, the architect stated that the extraordinary thick walls in the middle of the house dated from a period much older than the rest of the building, indicating that the new house had been built around the core of the old one.

Above: The Low House and Cruck Barn, Whirlow Hall Farm.

Left: The interior of the Cruck Barn 1977.

3

Many of the farming families had lived in Whirlow for generations taking on the tenancies of their fathers or fathers-in-law, marrying daughters of neighbouring farming stock with their descendants carrying on the line. The population was very small and it is likely that everyone knew everybody else. The farms and cottages were known by the names of the people who lived in them and this sometimes makes it difficult to track down who lived where. Many of the farming families had christian names which they passed down through the generations and this also makes for confusion, but there is no doubt that many of the Whirlow families lived there for over 200 years.

The land around Whirlow Hall rises to between 800 and 1,000 feet, the soil is mostly sandy loam and this, together with the high rainfall, produced good grassland ideal for sheep farming. The hillsides were full of springs and many areas required draining.

The old fields at Whirlow had been very large and possibly dated from the time they were claimed from woodland and moor. The Broom Fields, Rye Fields and Fenney Fields (Fenney is a dialect word for marshy) near Whirlow Hall were of a considerable size, but gradually over the years they were split into smaller units. No doubt the disadvantages of large fields had become apparent; there would be a lack of shelter in winter for the live stock and small fields made for more economical husbandry. Wheat, Rye and Plumtree Leys are old 18th Century field names which give some indication of the crops grown there.

Until the middle of the 19th Century, Whirlow remained a very rural area, the main land owners lived elsewhere, the farmers were mostly tenants, there would be little money to spare. It is against this background of a comparatively simple way of life that during the last part of the 19th Century, Whirlow witnessed the arrival of a totally different lifestyle, brought about by a new turnpike road, improved communications, air pollution in the city and the rise of the new steel magnates in Sheffield.

The building of the large houses in Whirlow attracted more wealth to the area — it became fashionable. After the First World War, more and more land was released for development, new houses began to creep along the old lanes and new roads too came into being.

Many of the these roads were to have Whirlow as part of their name and yet today there is no Whirlow Road. In the past there have been three Whirlow Roads, the old pack road, Fenney Lane, used by the packhorses as they travelled from Derbyshire to Sheffield, the Enclosure Road, part of which is now Broad Elms Lane and the Turnpike Road, now Ecclesall Road South.

After the Second World War with the cut backs in agriculture and the consequent reduction in the labour force, the close knit communities which had lived in the area for generations moved away. Some of the farms and cottages were purchased, not to be run as farms or small holdings, but for conversion and restoration.

4

As new houses were built the population grew and this pattern was to gain momentum as the 20th Century progressed. The ancient hamlet was to see many changes and before the old Whirlow fades from memory I have tried, together with photographs, to remind you of how it once was.

CHAPTER TWO

Broad Elms Lane...The Whirlow Road

BROAD Elms Lane is one of the very old roads of the district, it linked the ancient commons of Broad Oak Green and Whirlow Green. For a time it was a main thoroughfare before returning to a rural lane. As we shall see not only did it change its status but also its name. Strangely on some of the old maps it does not have a name at all and even on the Ordnance Survey map of 1854, the stretch of road we know today as Broad Elms Lane is not named, but one of its earlier names was the Whirlow Road.

The main routes of an area generally represent the roads, lanes and bridle ways that have been used for generations but others fall into disuse as more direct routes take their place. They become part of developed areas or field systems, relegated to folk-memory or ancient documents. As new thorough-fares are built, some old tracks lose their importance and become backwaters. As with other places this has happened too at Whirlow.

From the Limb Brook at Whirlow Bridge a hollow lane leads to Whirlow Hall and Broad Elms Lane; part of an ancient trackway, it is known as Fenney Lane. Now very overgrown, its high banks covered with foliage, this unmade road, worn down by generations of packhorses, is almost forgotten. But once it was a busy thoroughfare, the horses carrying their merchandise passing along on their way to Sheffield.

The Chapman Fields and Cross Fields on Broad Elms Lane are possible pointers to the way the packmen took. Chapmen were packmen or itinerant

Fenney Lane.
The old
Packhorse
Road.

traders. Cross Fields usually referred to the meeting point or crossing of roads. The route continued to Thrift House to join the old Saltway (Ringinglow Road) from Cheshire and up Psalter Lane to Sheffield. By 1855 the packhorse route above Alms Hill Farm had become a footpath. It is used to this day.

Coit Lane, a continuation of Fenney Lane above Whirlow Hall, now disappears into the fields, but its high hedges speak of an earlier time. At some stage this too must have joined the Ringinglow Road, perhaps near the Hoyle Houses (Castle Dyke Lodge) or Wigley Farm.

During the 18th Century the Duke of Devonshire endeavoured to make a new main highway into Sheffield. Trade was seriously threatened by inadequate roads and apart from the Saltway there were no main carriageways out west from Sheffield, only bridle paths and packhorse routes.

In 1750 the Duke's Steward gave notice that he hoped to make the lane past Whirlow Hall a high road. This was to cause much oppositon and anxiety in Whirlow where it was feared it would be a great inconvenience, would damage the fences and disturb the cattle and tenants. A great many ''ancient people'' were approached by the Hollis Trust, who owned part of the land. They affirmed that the road was not and never had been a public high road.

The people of Whirlow were to be spared this inconvenience until the 1788 Enclosure Award proclaimed that a public road to be called the Whirlow Road had been set out from Whirlow Green over Broad Oak Green to Carterknowle. This road encompassing Fenney Lane was to become, until the making of the Turnpike (Ecclesall Road South), the main parish road of the district.

During the Enclosures it was general practice for new fields to be edged with hawthorn or dry stone walls and the roads to have wide grass verges. Broad

Broad Elms Lane. Alms Vale Cottage is visible on the right.

Elms Lane is a very good example of an old enclosure road, the wide verges stipulated by the Enclosure Act only disappeared in the 1930's. The fields above Alms Hill still retain their walls and in spring are bright with May-blossom.

Around 1825, to avoid confusion with the new turnpike road, a portion of the Whirlow Road of the Enclosure changed its name to Broad Oak Lane, taking its name from the old common of Broad Oak Green and the oak tree planted there by the Broad Oak School in 1736.

Postal problems with other similarly named areas in Sheffield resulted in the name being changed yet again in 1903 to Broad Elms Lane.

The wonderful old photograph of Broad Elms Lane on the previous page taken in the early part of this century shows how rural the area still was. Bents Drive and Alms Hill Road were still to be built and in the distance on the left of the photograph we can see Broad Oak Farm.

BROAD OAK FARM

The earliest record is of Richard Crooke in 1669 when he was paying £4 per annum rent. George Redfearn was living there in 1717 when he was brought before the Ecclesall Manor Court for building a wall from his farm to the foot of Alms Hill, no doubt enclosing some extra fields. He was told to remove it! David Hancock was farming there in 1750. In 1819 Christopher Hancock rebuilt Broad Oak Farm, a stone over the door carried the date together with the initials C.H. The Hancocks lived at Broad Oak Farm for over 150 years.

Broad Elms Lane. Broad Oak School with Broad Oak Farm in the background, circa 1905.

(The Sheffield Postcard Co. Ltd.)

Broad Elms Lane. Broad Oak School and The Brush Factory showing the wide verges of the old Enclosure Road, circa 1900.

Benjamin, a file cutter, was the last Hancock to make his home there. They were a well known family whose relatives worked many of the local farms. They were also stone-masons and quarrymen. A Samuel Hancock helped to rebuild Castle Dyke in 1788/89. Samuel, a stone-mason was paid 2/4d per day and his son, Samuel, no doubt his apprentice, was paid 8d.

The Needhams were the last farmers of Broad Oak Farm. During the First World War it was necessary to cultivate as many fields as possible and when Mr. Needham ploughed the field across the road from the farm on Broad Elms Lane he found evidence that the game of Knur and Spell had been played there.

Knur and Spell is an ancient game vaguely resembling golf. It was played with a marble sized pottery or porcelain ball and a stick with a wooden block on its striking end. The winner was the man who drove the knur (the ball) the furthest distance in an agreed number of strikes. The knur was set for striking in a type of spring trap. It was these balls that Mr. Needham found as he ploughed the soil in readiness for a fine crop of oats.

With the advance of urban development in the 1920's and 30's and the building of new roads, Broad Oak Farm was the first on Broad Elms Lane to be demolished to make way for the building of Bents Drive.

BROAD OAK SCHOOL

Next to Broad Oak Farm was Broad Oak School together with its School House. This long stone building is now converted into four flats, but for nearly two hundred years it was a school. Founded as a Charity School in 1729, six poor boys or girls were to be taught English.

In 1841 three scholars were boarding at the school and by 1871 there were ten boarding pupils, two lodgers, two servants, the School Master, William Beet and his School Mistress wife, Sophia. It is said that in order to keep his

The Brush Factory, now Bents Green House, with the yew trees in the garden.

pupils healthy, Mr. Beet regularly gave his pupils monthly doses of Senna Tea! In the early part of this century the school became a mission hall, harvest festivals were held in the school room and the Mother's Union used it for their meetings. During the Second World War it became an A.R.P. Wardens' Post.

Around 1930 the Mission Hall once again became a school with Miss G. L. Jackson as Principal. Later Miss Hambley and Miss Givens ran the private school. Ecclesall High School maintained a high reputation and ran most successfully but in 1962 the two headmistresses and their eighty pupils were served with a notice to quit; the whole building required a great deal of money spending on it and the church, who owned the property, was forced to sell.

Today a bungalow stands on the school playground where generations of children played and three flats replace the garden where Miss Hambley and Miss Givens tended their roses.

THE BRUSH FACTORY

This tall three storey building with its unusual arched windows situated at the corner of Broad Elms Lane and Bents Road was built by Jonathan Makinson in 1828. Adjacent to it was a saw and timber yard. The wood was reputed to be stored under the arches, now the semi-circular windows. The cellar, now filled in, contained many millstones and a deep well whose water even in times of drought remained constant.

By 1841 Jonathan was making besoms, brushes made of twigs, tied around a handle. The twigs were often of heather readily available from the nearby moors. They were ideal for kitchen or garden use and had been made around this area for generations. In 1760 two dozen besoms cost 4/-.

The building had become two dwellings with the brush factory across the top which was approached by a stone staircase on the outside of the building.

Jonathan was said to be 6'6" tall, a Master Brush-maker, he lived here with his wife Mary, son Harry, a journeyman brush-maker, and two other sons, William and Jonathan. Next door lived Charles Makinson with his wife and his young son, Henry.

In 1871 Jonathan now 80 and a widower still lived here looked after by his son, Harry, now married with a stepson. Brushes were still being made. The factory consisted of three rooms running off a long corridor and the views from the windows were magnificent.

Joseph Vickers, a quarryman, lived next door with his wife Elizabeth and their six children. The second house was approached from the now blocked up doorway on Broad Elms Lane.

Later the house passed to the Mountford family from Abbey Lane and brush-making ceased.

The garden was much larger than it is today and Fred Mountford was justly proud of it. Creepers covered the house, the two large yew trees in the front garden still stand, but when Bents Road was widened, part of the frontage was lost and the yew trees are now on the pavement outside the garden wall. After her parents' death, Hannah Mountford remained in the house until her death at the age of 92.

On 16th November 1972 a preservation order was put on the old house and in 1975 it was converted into a maisonette and flat, the garden was sold for building and it also acquired a new name, Bents Green House.

ALMS VALE COTTAGE

Returning to the photograph on page 7, Alms Vale Cottage can be seen on the right hand side. When Henry Tatton drew this farm in 1932 he called it the

Sketch of Alms Vale Cottage by Henry Tatton 1932.   (Sheffield City Libraries)

11

Kennels. The locals called it Mrs. Barstow's but for many decades it was known as Alms Vale Cottage.

Originally there were two cottages with their gardens. In 1851 John Ibbotson, who made penknives, lived there with his wife Sarah, daughter Elizabeth and son William, who in time was to help his father in forging the penknife blades. Adam Hill, an apprentice cutler, also lived with them. Adam would probably have been apprenticed for seven years, an agreement having been made with his parents that the master would undertake to teach him his trade as well as providing him with food, clothing and lodging. For his part he would be bound to keep his master's secrets, obey his commands, remain single and generally behave in an orderly fashion. The penknives would probably have been made in a shop adjoining the cottage. Robert Wilson, a tailor, and his family lived in the other cottage.

The land was bounded by a stream, which when sold in 1878 was noted as having an almost unfailing source of water, very important in the days before piped water. This stream ran through the Brookfields down to Parkhead and it can still be seen today by Parkhead Post Office, before it is piped into a culvert under Ecclesall Road South.

CORKER'S NURSERY

During the 20th Century, the land adjacent and behind Alms Vale Cottage and running down to where Alms Hill Road is today was run as a nursery by

Above: Corker's Nursery looking towards Broad Elms Lane, circa 1952.

Right: Corker's Nursery. Parkhead Cottage is just visible on the right, circa 1952.

the Corker family. As seen in the photograph there were many glass houses and frames. Many of the plants flourishing in local gardens were purchased here. During the Second World War, land girls were employed at the nursery to assist in the war effort.

After the war Alms Vale Cottage was pulled down and a new house built on the land. The nurseries closed down in the 1960's and the land was sold for building.

A gennel ran down the side of the nursery from Broad Elms Lane to Parkhead. On the left hand side of the gennel was Parkhead Cottage, a delightful old house whose gardens were carpeted with bulbs in the spring. John Trippett was living there in 1798, but when Hill Turrets was developed in the 1960's, Parkhead Cottage was demolished to make way for new building.

ALMS HILL FARM

Alms Hill, Holms Hill and Holmes Hill are the names which have variously described the steep part of Broad Elms Lane. Holms is an old Norse word meaning settlement. In 1680 it was Horms Hill Top, by 1854 the Ordnance Survey map marked it as Alms Hill and for the next 120 years the farm situated on the left hand side of the lane was known as Alms Hill Farm. Today a group of houses on Broad Elms Close mark the spot. The small coppice is all that remains of the old farm and its buildings which were demolished in the 1970's.

Almshill Farm. Bends. Broad Elms Lane. The steps on the left lead to the field path to Thrift House. The steps on the right lead to the field path to Park Head. The house showing over the gate is the Turrets.

A sketch of Alms Hill Farm by Henry Tatton 1932. (Sheffield City Libraries)

Alms Hill Farm with Ivy Cottage 1959.

Joshua Storke was living at Horms Hill Farm, or Storke's house as it was called locally, in 1679, when a new chimney was erected at a cost of 13/2d. This original farm had been extended and now contained a "house", the old name for the main living room. There was also a parlour and buttery with bedrooms above and 87 feet of new glass.

Joshua Storke had some standing in the neighbourhood. In 1716 and for a number of years he provided the Manorial Court Dinners after the Easter and Michaelmas Courts had finished sitting. Did Sarah, his wife, use her mother-in-law's largest tablecloth left to her by Ellen Storke when she died in 1687 — it would certainly have proved useful on these occasions.

By 1725 John Dungworth Junior was farming at Holmes Hill Top, His descendant, another John, was still farming there in 1873. The Dungworths farmed many of the Whirlow farms. As we shall see they lived at Whirlow Hall, the Hall farm and at the farm on Whirlow Lane, now Gables Cottage.

In the 17th, 18th and 19th Centuries their name occurs time and again in the records. In 1756 John Dungworth, yeoman, was listed as one of the men holding free and common socage, that is to say they held free tenure without the obligation of military service. They were literate respected men, often witnesses to wills and appraisors of inventories, called in by executors after the death of a friend to value their goods and chattels.

There were many Dungworth brothers and sisters and many more Dungworth cousins. They lived in Whirlow for generations, marrying sons and

Sad pictures of Alms Hill Farm House and its barns, empty and forlorn, taken in June 1970.

15

daughters of neighbouring families. John, Joseph, Jonathan, Joshua, Samuel and Sarah were popular family names in all the Dungworth households.

Sarah and Samuel Dungworth rebuilt Alms House, as the farm was now called, in 1804. After Samuel's death, John, his son, took over the farm. John built a small cottage, Ivy Cottage, in the farm grounds for his widowed mother, Sarah, to live in. Ivy Cottage was a tiny picturesque house set beyond the barns and across the farm yard from the main house. For a time, Joseph, John's brother, ran the farm but by 1861 John, a widower, had returned together with his son, another John, and his wife Sarah. Alms Hill Farm house was not a large house but by 1871 John and Sarah had produced nine children, including another John and Sarah! The children's ages ranged from 2 months to 18 years, so it must have been a tight squeeze when they were all at home. The Dungworths remained at the farm until the 1890's when the Hulley family took over the tenancy.

The Hulleys were originally quarrymen. Jonathan Hulley had been foreman at the quarry at Whirlow Bridge in 1861. His son, John, ran the quarry before moving to Alms Hill Farm. Jonathan's descendants were not only to remain in possession of the farm but to become its last tenants. The vast changes that had taken place in agricultural life as machines took over from man and the ability to make far more money from the sale of land for building rang the death-knell for small farms. Mr. and Mrs. J. W. Hulley moved to Whirlow Lane Farm, and in the early 1970's Fitzwilliam Estates put Alms Hill Farm on the market. Just below the site of the old farm the old stone trough remains. When W. H. Mander painted his picture of this old trough around 1894 (see frontispiece) he called the beauty spot Alms Hill near Sheffield, reminding us that this was still the countryside, an area far removed from the town. When piped water first arrived at the local farms in 1933 the cattle wouldn't drink it and they had to be taken back to the troughs for their drinking water. The water in the area was considered to be very pure and the water that flowed through the troughs at Thrift House was locally acknowledged to be a "cure-all": sick children were often given a glass of it to cure their ills.

Until the advent of piped water for those cottages without a well, water had to be carried from pond or stream. In Whirlow the water flowing through the

The Old Stone Trough, Alms Hill.

Alms Hill in 1915. The steps on the left led to the field path to Thrift House.

streams was collected by the householders from a series of troughs which were fed by natural gravity. In time it was necessary to supplement the streams and a reservoir was constructed near Thrift House. This "reservoir" now a small lake, makes a desirable feature in the garden of a house on Ringinglow Road.

The fields on the right hand side of the lane where the modern Broad Elms School is situated were known as the "roughs". In summer the boggy areas at the bottom were carpeted with flowers, in the autumn there were large juicy blackberries to be picked and in the winter it was a wonderful area for sledging. In the early part of this century these fields were used as a rifle range. As a boy at Alms Hill Farm, Mr. Hulley used to go with his friends to collect the spent lead pellets.

The steps in the photograph opposite to Alms Hill Farm led to the field path to Thrift House. There was another path lower down the lane which ran across the fields to Plumpton Cottages, then out through the Spout Field to Ringinglow Road.

In earlier times in the fields behind Alms Hill Farm were two "foot-roads" which led to a quarry in the Knowle Fields. By 1860 this quarry was being worked out. There had been a quarry too behind Broad Oaks School and old gravel pits on Whirlow Lane and near Thrift House. Provision had been made at the time of the Enclosure Award in 1788 for various stone quarries to be used for building purposes, one of these was on Haugh Lane. In the 1920's the first modern houses were built, but still a large portion of the lane remained comparatively rural and even today high above the lane near the drinking trough on Alms Hill, part of the old causeway still remains, the stone slabs a reminder of a bygone age.

The old path leading from Alms Hill to Plumpton. Part of the wall in the sketch by Henry Tatton still remains.
(Sheffield City Libraries).

18

CHAPTER THREE

Whirlow Hall

SOME of the earliest documents of Whirlow apply to the Bright family of Whirlow Hall. Many local historians have already written about the Brights, but it is necessary when writing about Whirlow to once again set down some of the details of the family who lived at Whirlow Hall for centuries.

Early records can be very confusing and it is difficult to pinpoint when the family first settled in Whirlow. In Hunter's *Hallamshire* there is mention of a deed of 1303 by which Robert de Ecclesall, Lord of the Manor of Ecclesall, gave some lands in Whirlow, the Hall and several messuages to the tenant then in possession, one John Bright, possibly the same John of Whirlow of 1341 mentioned in the Introduction. But there is another document of 1410 which states that John Stephenson mortgaged a messuage called "Horlowe Hall" and several lands in Whirlow to John Bright for 100 marks (a mark was 13/4d, two thirds of a £1). This is all rather puzzling, but it would seem that the Brights were living in Whirlow in 1410 and possibly for over a hundred years before that.

Richard Bright was making arrowheads in Whirlow in the reign of Henry VII; as we shall see there were still the remains of a long disused smithy at Whirlow Hall in 1938. The English long-bow was recognised as a fearsome weapon, the arrows, fletched with goose feathers, having a vicious steel point. Although the use of bows and arrows had begun to decline after the end of the

Whirlow Hall Farm.

19

War of the Roses in 1485, they were still used both for military purposes and for hunting. Crossbows were used by the gentry in the 16th Century to kill the deer in Ecclesall Woods. By 1571 the Brights were a well established yeoman family, freeholders, farming their own land. John, Henry and Thomas were popular family names carried down through the generations.

It was the John Bright who died in 1586, who was the founder of the complicated family dynasty that ensued from the marriage of his three sons, Henry, Thomas and John, to the daughters of neighbouring yeomen families. Their progeny were to people many of the large houses in and around the area and their influence was to be far reaching.

In 1638 John Bright's grandson, Stephen, obtained by dubious means the Manor and Lordship of Ecclesall. The Manor passed down from Stephen through a rather tenuous line of descent to Mary Bright of Badsworth who in 1752 married Charles Wentworth, the second Marquis of Rockingham. When he died in 1782 the Manor of Ecclesall which contained a good deal of Whirlow land, passed to his heir, his nephew Earl Fitzwilliam, and consequently much of Whirlow became an outpost of a great estate.

In most great families, records and archives are kept. It is indeed fortunate that one of the descendants of yeoman Bright of Whirlow Hall married into one such family and that so many of the documents and papers of the Bright family, which might normally have been destroyed, were retained.

The Brights were to remain in possession of Whirlow Hall, its lands and farms until a virtually bankrupt Henry Bright parted with the estate to Sir John Statham around 1720. The Bright family had made a great deal of their money from lead smelting. In the 16th Century lead had become a very important commodity; Elizabethan England was experiencing a building boom and lead was in great demand for roofing, gutters, cisterns, etc. Many of the important families of Derbyshire and Sheffield were engaged in the industry and the Brights were no exception. Lead was readily available in Derbyshire, wood for smelting was obtained in Ecclesall Woods and the packhorse routes to Sheffield and Bawtry were nearby. The lead was carried down the river Idle to Stockwith on to Hull for export to London and the continent.

With their considerable holding of moorland, it is reasonable to suppose that the Brights were also sheep farmers. In Tudor England the cloth trade was the major industry, wool was fetching very high prices, and the Brights would wish to take advantage of this prosperity. They continued to prosper and the money was ploughed back into land and property.

At the corner of Fenney Lane and Whirlow Lane, sheltered by a bank of sycamore trees, stands an old farm house, built in 1843, it is the descendant of the once ancestral house of the Bright family, Whirlow Hall.

The previous Hall was reputed to have been built in Elizabethan times by the Bright family, similar in style to the one they built at Banner Cross. A sketch of the old Hall in *The Manor and Parish of Ecclesall* by Carolus Paulus shows a stone-faced building with mullioned and transomed windows. Some of the

Whirlow Hall, the new "Hall" built in 1843.

rooms were reputed to have been very large, one nine yards wide was said to contain a window with 470 panes of glass, no doubt small ones. A fire-place had a date stone of 1619. The Hall had probably been a timber framed hall house, additions and rebuilding in stone could possibly account for the date stone. Much rebuilding was taking place in Yorkshire at this time, as prosperous yeomen wished to improve their houses. Henry Bright's marriage

The sketch by W. Farnsworth of Old Whirlow Hall which appears in The Manor and Parish of Ecclesall by Carolus Paulus.

21

settlement of 1655 gives us some indication of its size. After his marriage his father was to retain the west wing of the Hall for his own use, together with several barns, out-houses, stables and a garden. It was obviously a house befitting a man of status.

The Bright family had been living at Whirlow for many generations when Henry's son, another Henry, inherited the estate in 1694. When his father married in 1655, the estate stretched far beyond Whirlow and Fulwood and their original holding of 1410. He inherited lands in Whirlow, Ecclesall, Fulwood, Ecclesfield and elsewhere in Yorkshire. There was land in Derbyshire, many houses, orchards, woodlands and moorland. However this Henry was to be a very different character from his forebears. According to Hunter's *Hallamshire* his fondness for high living was to bring his family to virtual ruin. Henry began to sell land and property. There are records of mortgages taken out on the estate as a means of raising money. Some of the estate was sold to other members of the Bright family.

With his financial position becoming increasingly precarious, Henry began to divide the Hall and lease sections to various tenants. The land so diligently amassed by his ancestors was dissipated. With his ever increasing debts it became necessary around 1720 to part with the Hall and the remnants of the estate to Sir John Statham of Tideswell. Although Henry was to be the last Bright of Whirlow Hall, another branch of the family, Sir John Bright of Badsworth had inherited the Manor of Ecclesall from his father, Stephen, and they now owned large areas of land and property in Whirlow. Sir John died in 1688, his estate passing to his grandson, another John. In 1725 John Bright commissioned John Gelley to survey his land in Ecclesall, the map that he produced showed the extensive holding owned by John Bright in Whirlow.

From this time this once ancestral home was to become tenanted, its owners residing elsewhere. Together with Whirlow Hall Farm it was still one of the largest in the area, but with the loss of its powerful owners its status became diminished. Whirlow Hall as it had once been, was gone for ever.

1725-1842

Although Sir John Statham had purchased the Whirlow Hall estate he was not to retain it for long, for on 6th October 1725 the Court Leet of Ecclesall recognised that Thomas Hollis had purchased the Hall, the farm, Whirlow Mill and 146 acres of land for £1,900. In 1726 the Hollis family gave the Whirlow land to the Hollis Trust. These lands and properties were to be supervised by the Trustees of the Hollis Trust who still own land and property in Whirlow today.

Thomas Hollis did not wish to live in the Hall himself and he continued the process, started by Henry Bright, of converting it into dwellings, spending £200 on the conversion. This once proud Hall had become in reality nothing more than a series of apartments.

In 1725 John Dungworth became a tenant. The Dungworths were to remain in possession of the Hall until Mary Dungworth married William Furness in 1843 when he took over the tenancy.

In 1739 the Dungworths were given permission to carry out repairs and to build a dairy. By 1742 John and his brother appeared to be tenanting the whole of the Hall and the adjacent farm.

The Hall was obviously very old and becoming more and more dilapidated. Samuel Shore, a Trustee of the Hollis Trust, writing to Timothy Hollis in London in 1785 wrote "that the dwelling houses at Whirlow Hall of which there are three, as well as the out-buildings and the walls about the place are in much disorder and it will take a considerable sum of money to put them all in due repair, the roofs of several of the buildings are bad". Permission was given to repair just the Hall on the understanding that the tenants kept it in better order in the future. The Dungworths, although good at looking after the land, had obviously done little to keep the farms and out-buildings in good repair. They had also displeased the Trustees by not looking after the woodlands, a valuable source of revenue.

These repairs were only to prolong the Hall's life for a short time for in 1795 the east wing was pulled down. According to Hunter's *Hallamshire* the remainder was later demolished, but local legend recalls that it was struck by lightning and burnt down.

1843

A new house was to arise where the old one had been, not as pretentious as the old Hall, but nevertheless a fine dwelling without the problems that must have existed in the ancient building that preceded it. It must have been an exciting time for Mary Dungworth, newly married to William Furness, when they became the first tenants of the new "Hall".

By 1851 William had begun to manufacture scythes, in conjunction with running the farm. A journalist writing in the *Sheffield Telegraph* in 1938 remarks on seeing at Whirlow Hall "the long disused bellows and the stone on which the anvil stood". In 1853 William took over the tenancy of the Whirlow Wheel at Whirlow Bridge which was retained in the family until 1913.

William Furness was the son of Richard Furness, the schoolmaster of Dore, of whom much has been written elsewhere. William was well educated. He was interested in politics and local history and his knowledge of Whirlow was considerable. Both the Rev. Cobby and S. O. Addy, notable historians of their day, pay tribute to the contribution he made to the knowledge of the area. William's second son, Richard, took over the Hall on his father's death in 1895.

As a child Molly Grayson, née Clark, remembered the bonfire parties held at the Hall. She also remembered the valuable furniture. As a small girl it seemed to her black and rather heavy, but on Richard's death in 1928 it was

The pigeon loft.

sent to Christie's in London to be sold — quite an unusual occurrence at that time.

Richard's son, John William, was to be the last Furness of Whirlow Hall. Like his grandfather, his local knowledge of Whirlow and Ecclesall was considerable. He could remember Whirlow when his grandfather thought nothing of walking to Cheshire on business. The farmer used to go to Sheffield in the horse and cart to take the butter and eggs to market. Eggs were sixteen for 1/-, beer 3d per pint. They also supplied the large houses in the area with hay for the horses. As a young man, Mr. Furness earned 21/- per week. When Walter Clarke took over the tenancy of Whirlow Hall in 1937, Mr. Furness moved to Whirlow Farm, so bringing to an end, after two hundred years, the occupancy of Whirlow Hall by the Furness family and their ancestors, the Dungworths.

Behind the Hall was a small stone rectangular building, a pigeon loft. Pigeons and doves were a useful source of fresh meat in wintertime and their manure was highly valued. Until the early part of the 20th Century there were hive stones in the garden. Made of stone, they acted as a base for straw beehives. The Hall also boasted a fine sundial, a relic from the old Hall. The late Mr. Furness remembered two old stones in the garden wall dated 1619, the same date as the fireplace in the old Hall but sadly, like the hive-stones, these have now disappeared. The curious stone carving of a face on the wall in the farm yard was reputed to have been sculptored by Richard Furness, the father of the first William Furness — it came from Dore Chapel.

After the Second World War, Mr. Dennis Merryweather who was then living at Whirlow Hall landscaped the lovely gardens in the photograph.

Just below the Hall is the Hall Farm or Low House, now a listed building. It is one of the oldest farms in the area dating back to the 17th Century. The cruck barns are possibly older and justly famous. Carolus Paulus writing in

24

The Low House and landscaped gardens of Whirlow Hall.

1927 mentioned two oak doors in the barns which were dated 1652, but these too have disappeared.

1979

In 1979 Whirlow Hall took on a new role as a working farm for the school children of Sheffield. Leased from the City Council, who acquired Whirlow Hall Farm in 1943 and Whirlow Hall in 1949, the farm is administered by the Whirlow Hall Farm Trust, a charitable organisation.

Today education and farming run side by side; needy and handicapped children visit Whirlow Hall Farm to learn about animals and their needs and

Traditional Well-Dressing of The Farm Well 1981.

life on a farm. Princess Anne visited in 1980 and saw for herself how the needs of the handicapped child were being met in this new venture. In 1983 dormitories were opened in Whirlow Hall itself to give children the opportunity of living and learning in a rural and historic setting.

William and Mary Furness moving into Whirlow Hall in 1843 would have found it difficult to visualise the vast changes that were to take place on their farm in the 20th Century. From the age of the horse to one of mechanisation was a tremendous leap forward. The pace of life quickened as elsewhere; it was even more dramatic as machines took over from men and a large labour force was no longer required to work the farm.

But the sense of history remains and when the children return home the old mellow buildings of Whirlow Hall Farm are a reminder that men have lived and worked there through all the changes, for nearly 600 years.

CHAPTER FOUR

Whirlow Green . . . Horlowe Green

NESTLING at the corner of Broad Elms Lane and Whirlow Lane are an old farm and a group of cottages which together with a green and two ponds were known as Whirlow Green. Today the green and the ponds have gone, but Whirlow Farm and the cottages remain.

The green stretched along Broad Elms Lane and down Whirlow Lane opposite the farm, one pond was in front of Whirlow Farm cottages, the other is shown on the photograph of Whirlow Green. The ponds provided a useful additional source of water for Whirlow Hall and the nearby cottages before the days of piped water. Tubs, milk-churns and vats were used to carry the water, a hard back-breaking task.

When the cottages were built they faced away from the lane for extra security. The farm and the cottages were approached by the drive from Whirlow Lane. Although the cottages had their own gardens, they looked on to an enclosed farm yard.

Whirlow Farm and the cottages at Whirlow Green have a long history. Elizabeth Sheldon was living here in 1646. She was followed by the Machons, whose family were to lease the farm from the Brights for the next hundred years. By 1748 Joseph Machon was old and poor and no doubt a liability; for some time on the orders of Mr. Bright, Mr. Battie, his steward, had been giving him money. In 1749 they came to an arrangement whereby if Joseph was prepared to give up the tenancy, Mr. Bright would pay him an allowance of £2 per annum. This was agreed and Sam Clarke, whose family lived nearby, took over the tenancy.

It is difficult to tell when the Clarke family first arrived at Whirlow but they were to work many of the local farms. Francis Clarke was farming at Whirlow Lane Farm in 1725 and when Samuel Clarke moved to Whirlow Farm, he became one of a long line of the same family to live at the farm, until their descendant, Walter Clark(e), left to take over Whirlow Hall in 1937.

By 1841 a file shop had been added to one of the Whirlow Farm cottages. Alexander Barker lived here with his wife Mary and six of the eight children that Mary was to bear him. Sadly Mary appears to have died before her 50th birthday. Alex's father lived down the lane at Broad Oak Green where there was also an old cutler's shop, so possibly he had served his apprenticeship there. His sons too carried on the tradition for by 1851 three of them, Samuel, William and Alex junior, were apprenticed to their father.

The file smiths generally collected sufficient blanks for a week's work. When finished, the files were put into a roll of cloth for protection and then returned to Sheffield, generally on a Saturday, where they were sold.

Reflections in the Pond at Whirlow Green, circa 1905.

Whirlow Farm originally the home of the Clarke family.

28

As the years went by the Clarke boys were also employed in the local metal industry. In the summer when there was a great deal of work on the farm, all the young men would be required to lend a hand with the work at Whirlow Farm. The late Molly Grayson, Walter Clarke's daughter, remembered a gin-race at the farm. This was used to grind the corn. The millstone was turned by a donkey. All the farmers knew the fields by their names and although most of them were near the farm, sometimes there were some in the tenancy some distance away. This was the case at Whirlow Farm, where two fields called the Lawns were situated adjacent to Ecclesall Woods, where Whirlow Park Road is today. For generations the farmers had taken their cows to the Lawns to graze. They were taken down Whirlow Lane across the road to an old green lane which remained until the 20th century, but is virtually unknown to modern Whirlow. Share Lane was marked on Gelley's map of 1725 and before the making of the turnpike road, Ecclesall Road South, it was a continuation of Croft Lane. Adjacent to Whirlow Court it was for many years part of that estate, having been conveyed by Earl Fitzwilliam in 1907. Eventually in the 1970's the lane was taken into the gardens of Whirlow Grove and all trace of its existence disappeared. As we shall see with Rose Cottage, Whirlow Farm Cottages were put up for sale in July 1978. The file shop had long since gone and agricultural needs had diminished. The two cottages were sold and converted into a single residence; the front door no longer facing inwards but out towards Whirlow Lane.

Whirlow Farm Cottages, before conversion.

Rose Cottage, June 1915.

In 1977 a move was made to protect Whirlow Green by making it a conservation area. In October the City Council's environmental projects committee approved the scheme and it was subsequently passed by the South Yorkshire County Council. The buildings were scheduled as being of historical and architectural interest, Grade II.

ROSE COTTAGE

Rose Cottage too faced away from the lane. Possibly this was not only for protection but also for warmth. Before the days of central heating and with the prevailing wind sweeping down from the high moors, it would be warmer to have the cottage facing this way.

The cottage was approached by a gennel, which ran up the lower side of the small holding round to the original front door and then on to the back of Whirlow Farm.

Below the cottage are the Tenter Meadows. In earlier times these were small fields where cloth was hung to be stretched and bleached. The manufacture of woollen cloth was widespread in South Yorkshire in the 16th and 17th Centuries. There were linen weavers living at Whirlow in 1650, so possibly linen cloth or harden, a coarse hard cloth used for aprons and bed linen, was to be found hanging in the Tenter Meadows.

The Tenter Meadows.

In the 17th Century there were the Rose Fields at Whirlow. Dog roses still grow in the hedgerows, so perhaps this is how this cottage became to be known as Rose Cottage. In 1978 the last farm labourer moved out of the two bedroomed cottage and Fitzwilliam Estates put the property on the market. In 1980 a new Rose Cottage emerged, completely modernised and considerably enlarged, with a new wing of bedrooms and garages erected at the side.

CHAPTER FIVE

Whirlow Lane and Little Common Lane

WALKING down from Whirlow Green to the Rising Sun on Abbey Lane it is hard to imagine the many changes that have taken place on this ancient way. Before the making of Turnpike (Ecclesall Road South) which bisected it in 1816, Whirlow Lane and Little Common Lane were all one lane which joined together two old routes of Whirlow, the Whirlow Road (Broad Elms Lane) and Abbey Lane. It was called Little Common Road in 1807 and although by 1854 it had been cut in two, both parts were known as Whirlow Lane. By 1903 the area from Ecclesall Road South to Abbey Lane had become known as Little Common Lane.

The photograph taken in 1969 shows the gate to Whirlow Lane Farm and the three old stone cottages situated below the farm where Whirlow Lane meets Croft Lane.

In 1971 these cottages were served with a clearance order as they were considered unfit for habitation. A group of Whirlow residents together with the Hallamshire Historic Buildings Society endeavoured to save them. Although they were given six months' reprieve in the hope that someone would come forward with a satisfactory solution, it was not to be and they were demolished.

Entrance to Whirlow Lane Farm 1969.

Croft Lane Cottages 1969.

Whirlow Lane Farm, Winter 1977.

34

The farmhouse of Whirlow Lane Farm, like so many of the other Whirlow farms, was a rebuild of a much older house. There is a dwelling marked here on Gelley's map of 1725. When Mr. and Mrs. J. Hulley left Alms Hill Farm they took over the tenancy from Mr. Thomas Coates. They were to be the last farmers of Whirlow Lane Farm. With the continuing cut back in small farms Fitzwilliam Estates decided to sell and it was put on the market in May 1977.

Fortunately the need for conserving the old stone buildings had been realised, they were no longer being demolished so readily. At Whirlow Lane Farm there was not only an attractive farmhouse but an extensive group of out-buildings, pig styes, loose boxes, etc., together with over half an acre of land. It was ideal for conversion.

The farm was sympathetically converted into five very attractive cottages. Whirlow Farm Mews has won several awards for the skilful way in which it was developed.

Old Farm Buildings on Whirlow Lane.

The old buildings on Whirlow Lane are all on the same side of the road where it is more sheltered; it wasn't until the 20th Century that houses began to appear on the other side of the road. In 1919 Samuel Doncaster drew up plans for a new four bedroomed house and in 1920 further additions to include two turret rooms were proposed. Ellerburn (Greenway) was the first of these new houses to be built but gradually more houses began to edge their way along the old lane. The area was still very rural, the fields at the back stretching away to Alms Hill Farm and on to Thrift House. For many years Greenway was the home of Norman Thornton, of Thorntons, the chocolate manufacturers, and his family.

The cluster of buildings that face on to Ecclesall Road South belie their age. Originally they were farms and cottages lived in by some of the old farming families of Whirlow. The stone outbuildings on the corner of Whirlow Lane and Croft Lane are reminders that this was once a croft farmed for generations by the Dungworths. In May 1701 John Dungworth married Sarah Fowler. I think it is quite possible John married the girl next door, for Henry Fowler farmed the croft adjacent to the Dungworths. In time John and Sarah's son, John, took over both holdings. It was customary for the tenants of the Lord of the Manor, given his approval, to be succeeded by their sons from generation to generation, and this seems to have been the case in Whirlow where the same families were dwelling on the same land in some cases for centuries.

William Dungworth married Hannah Lee of Thrift House; two of their sons were cutlers, but Samuel, a farmer succeeded his father. Mary, William's daughter, remained a spinster; she returned to her mother's old house at Thrift House where she farmed until she died in 1859.

By 1851 Sam Dungworth was becoming an old man. His wife, Sarah, appears to have died and his young grandson and grandaughter, Thomas and Fanny, had moved in to help their grandfather run the croft. In due course Thomas married, and he and his wife, Mary Ann, took over the farm.

The Fowlers were living in Whirley Lane in the 17th Century. We know from building accounts of 1680 that their home comprised a house, the name for the main living room which generally contained a hearth, a buttery and a parlour. The parlour was often the principal bedroom and the chambers if any were used for storage. The ground floor was paved with stone flags, a great improvement on the earth floors of the past. Window tax in 1725 was levied on Henry Fowler at 2/-, which generally indicated a small house with less than ten windows.

In the Introduction I mentioned the substantial alterations carried out on some of the Whirlow farms in 1679/80. Several, including Henry Fowler's, had new roofs of slates (stone tiles) which came from the quarry at Alms Hill. Henry who participated in some of this work forwarded his account to Mr. Cook "for loading 4 hundreds of slate from Orms Hill 2/6d".

Although the Fowler holding passed to the Dungworth family around 1743, a hundred years later this parcel of land, now The Gables, was still referred to as the Fowler Croft.

The farms and cottages situated between Croft Lane and Whirlow Lane had their land chopped in two by the Turnpike road, although they still retained the portion of land that remained south of the road. It must have given rise to many problems not only with the loss of part of their holding, but with the fencing and grazing of their animals.

WHIRLOW CROFT

Whirlow Croft was not built at the time of the other fine houses on Ecclesall Road South; originally a farm house it is part of a much older Whirlow.

Whirlow Croft 1928.

Without the benefit of postal addresses, it is difficult to pinpoint with 100% accuracy exactly where people lived in the 16th Century, but it is quite possible that it was here that John Fisher of Whorlowe Lane was living before his death in April 1557. John was a man of substance; he and his wife, Elizabeth, had six children, three girls and three boys. The three girls, Elizabeth, Alice and Marie, together with his wife received the bulk of his estate. There were many clauses in his will, but it is the bequest to his three little boys, Thomas, Robert and Edward, his younger children, that immediately conjures up the past. They were each to receive a doublet. Suddenly we are back in Tudor England, to the last year of the reign of Mary Tudor, to the time of doublet and hose. In Gelley's Fieldbook of 1725, another John Fisher is recorded as tenant. The Fishers were followed by the Burrows family and then the Gills.

The changing face of Ecclesall Road South at the end of the 19th Century was also to transform Whirlow Croft. The Dixon family purchased from Earl Fitzwilliam in 1893 not only Whirlow Croft, but the two dwellings next door and the adjacent farm. They now leased a large parcel of land from Earl Fitzwilliam bordering Whirlow Lane, Croft Lane and Ecclesall Road South. Whirlow Croft was purchased not for use as a farm house, but for conversion into a house of some importance in keeping with the other large houses that were being built nearby.

Not only was the house updated, but gardens too were landscaped. Backhouse of York, one of the foremost nurserymen of their day, were engaged to build a rock garden. A tennis court and later a fives court were built; even today that would be quite an innovation. Edward Dixon sold Whirlow Croft in 1915, but he was not moving far, for when Edgar Allen died and Whirlow House was put on the market, he bought it.

The small estate was sold in two Lots — Lot 1 consisted of Whirlow Croft, a garage for three cars — quite novel in 1915 — stabling for two horses and a coal and stick house. Lot 2 consisted of a pair of substantial dwelling houses, a compact farmstead with house, cowhouse, piggeries, stables, loose-box, farm yard and paddock. It is also noted in the sale plan that planted in the grounds were yews of a great age, giving further substance and proof of its ancient lineage.

In July 1928 the two substantial stone dwellings of Lot 2 were purchased by Mr. Hubert C. Nicholson. He converted them into one large house which he called The Gables. The Nicholsons were a local family. J. W. Nicholson, Hubert's father, was a well known Sheffield stockbroker. As a child Hubert had lived at Plumpton near Thrift House, his father having moved there from Dickfield House at Little Common. When his sister, Maude, was married in 1909 the reception was held at Plumpton and the large field in front of the house was filled with horse-drawn carriages. In those days before the building of Bents Drive, Plumpton, which is one of the oldest houses in the area, was approached by a lane from Ringinglow Road.

Hubert's father left Plumpton in 1927 and purchased Whirlow Croft from Mrs. Wild. Hubert was to follow his father there in 1933 and his brother, A. W. Nicholson, took over The Gables. Later he too was to live at Whirlow Croft.

LITTLE COMMON LANE

During the end of the 18th Century and the beginning of the 19th Century this was the industrial area of Whirlow, not perhaps as we think of industry today, but nevertheless a busy lively area.

For generations the men of Whirlow had been small farmers, eking out an existence from the soil and the husbanding of their animals. The great contrast between moorland and forest that existed in the area widened the scope of activity for the people who lived and worked there. In the early years it was mainly a pastoral community, but the proximity of Ecclesall Woods provided not only pasturage, but wood for building and for charcoal and oak bark for tanning. In 1624 the Cutlers' Company was formed in Sheffield. To a very large extent the cutlery and tool trade was a domestic one; by building a shop and smithy adjacent to the farm the farmer could follow this new trade when work on the farm became slack in winter and when the harvest was over.

In 1726 the Cutlers' Company recorded that many thousands of men were employed in the secondary metal industry in Hallamshire. In time Whirlow men too became actively engaged in one form of tool-making or another; by the end of the 18th Century and the beginning of the 19th Century they were combining farming and metal working. The farmers' sons became apprenticed to their fathers or the farmer/cutler down the lane.

THE FARMERS/METAL WORKERS

Scythes were made at Whirlow Hall, files at Whirlow Green, pen-knives at Broad Elms, but the main area of the metalwork industry was on Little Common Lane and Abbey Lane. In 1787 Sampson Brookshaw was making pocket knives; later as landlord of the Rising Sun he was to carry on both occupations. Subsequent landlords followed his example: William Loukes in 1814 was making pen-knives and in 1861 George Thorpe was grinding scythes.

John Hallam was making scythes on Little Common Lane in 1825. By 1861 John Cox had taken over the business and his ancestors were still making them in 1938. The Cox family lived at Woodville. When the scythe works were sold in 1939, Mr. H. Mottram, the builder, purchased Woodville, the scythe works and all the adjoining cottages.

The scythe works were converted, the upper floor into a flat and offices, the ground floor into a large garage and storage area. One of the cottages was demolished to enable the builders' vehicles to enter the yard at the back. For

The converted Scythe Works, Little Common Lane 1978.

39

The Scythe Grinders Cottages, Little Common Lane, circa 1905.

a number of years the tiny end cottage was uninhabited; the photograph shows the scythe grinders' cottages as they were around 1905. In 1984 the demolished cottage was in effect replaced and all the cottages converted into one residence.

THE TANNERS

Mary Bramhill in her book *How they lived in Old Ecclesall* mentions the Hallatts of Little Common. They were farming at Little Common in 1678 and were still living there when Lucy Hallatt married Charles Hallatt, a farmer from Baslow in 1857. They lived at Dickfield.

By 1706 the Hallatts had also become tanners. The tan-yard is marked on Fairbank's map of 1760. It was near to where St. Luke's Hospice is today. The tan-yard contained a small building for dressing leather. It was some distance from the farm — tanning was a smelly business! It was also an important industry. Garments were made from leather, so too were bellows, belts for grinding, sheaths for knives and many other articles in common usage at that time. Tanning preserved the leather and made it waterproof.

Sheffield tanners were importing hides from Smithfield Market in London as early as 1646; they came via the Humber and Bawtry to Sheffield. Oak bark played an essential role in tanning. It was stripped from the tree in spring before the tree was felled. The bark was beaten and crushed into pieces. The leather was soaked in pits filled with water and the crushed oak bark. John Hallatt did not have far to go for his bark — Ecclesall Woods with their fine oaks lay just across the field from the tan-yard. In John Bright's account book for 1730 there are records of Thomas Allott (Hallatt), John's son, paying 10/6d and again in 1739 £1.4s.0d for the "bark of the said trees".

By 1841 all mention in the records of the tannery had gone. William Hallatt had returned to farming. His son, Alexander, was also farming and his twin sons, Samuel and Charles, had become tool makers and joiners. But in folk memory the tannery lived on — one elderly citizen who died in 1985 used to refer to Dickfield House as 'the old tan-yard'.

CHANGING TIMES

When my childen were small in the early 1960's we used to walk down Little Common Lane. Although vehicular access was then possible from Ecclesall Road South, it was a backwater, a quiet rural lane, very different from the old industrial lane of earlier times. Dickfield House with the farm and cottages lay on the right. We used to pat the horse and look at the pigs. There were just two other cottages at the bottom of the lane which belonged to Clifford House. The scythe grinders' cottages, the old scythe works together with Woodville Cottage, lay behind the Rising Sun on the left.

Times were to change on Little Common Lane once again. For a long time the people of Sheffield had been in need of a special hospital for the relief of the terminally ill. In 1967 a group of people got together to raise the money to build one such hospital. British Steel, who owned Clifford House, and whose land bordered Little Common Lane, gave two acres of this land on

Little Common Lane 1977.

41

which to build the hospice. In October 1971 St. Luke's Hospice opened with its first patients.

In 1980 half an acre of land adjacent to Dickfield farm was sold. New houses grew where the old farm buildings used to be. Further development took place and by this time the approach from Ecclesall Road South had been blocked to cars, access was only possible for pedestrians.

If approached from Ecclesall Road South, the first few yards are the old original lane, its edges bordered by holly trees. Holly trees have been growing around Little Common Lane for centuries. In earlier times holly was grown as a crop. It was farmed to feed the sheep in winter. The holly was often coppiced, the trunks cut at the base to allow for regeneration from the stumps that remained. It was a tradition in Hallamshire for the shepherds to cut the holly on Boxing Day, the sheep finding the fresh leaves and shoots highly desirable. The area in which holly was grown for this purpose was known as the Hollins — there were fields near Little Common Lane and Abbey Lane, known as Hollins, Little Hollings and Great Hollings.

CHAPTER SIX

Abbey Lane

ABBEY Lane in 1728, Bushey Croft Lane in 1807, Little Common or Common Lane in 1854 and Wood Lane by the local people, different names for the same road, the road we know today as Abbey Lane.

Abbey Lane is another of the ancient lanes of the area. It was very much narrower than it is today, the wood coming to the edge of the lane on the left hand side of the road as it ran down to the yet unbuilt Whirlowdale Road. In 1904 there were just two dwellings on this side of the lane, Wellfield House, usually known as Mountford's Farm, and Brackenhurst, the house of Mr. Charles Doncaster. Cow Lane above Brackenhurst went into the wood as it does today.

Wellfield House is marked on Gelley's map of 1725. In 1770 Abraham Hill was living there followed by his son, John. By 1817 Thomas Garfitt had moved into the farm. In common with many of the other local farmers, he turned part of the farm into a workshop for making files and ten years later he added a smithy. In a directory of 1825 he is recorded as a file maker and in 1833 as a scythe maker.

Around 1823 Mr. Garfitt's daughter, Hannah, married George Mountford. In 1840 they tenanted the Totley Scythe Forge. Their four children, Emma, George, Frederick and Benjamin were all born in Totley. In 1856 the scythe forge was sold and possibly as a result of this, Hannah and George moved with their children to Wellfield House. Certainly by 1861 they were farming

Abbey Lane with Wellfield Farm on the right, circa 1905. The Farm and the cottages have all been demolished.

Wellfield Farm Scythe Works, circa 1900. Mr. Mountford with the scythe smiths.

and making scythes there, helped by their two sons, George, now 19, and Fred, 16.

Fred Mountford married and eventually moved with his family to the Brush Factory on Bents Road. In the photograph he can be seen wearing a suit and a bowler hat. Benjamin carried on the farm at Wellfield House and Fred, helped by his son, Oliver, ran the scythe works.

The Mountfords continued with their joint enterprise until Abbey Lane was widened and the scythe works were pulled down. The business moved to Sheffield, taking the name of the farm with it. "Wellfield Works" began a new era at Mary Street in 1907.

Wellfield House, Abbey Lane, reverted to farming once again and continued to do so until it was demolished in the 1960's. The stone from the farm was used to build one of the new houses which replaced it.

LITTLE COMMON

In 1587 the area around the Rising Sun was known as Little Common. It covered just two acres, a small triangular piece of common land it stretched from Little Common Lane to Wellfield Farm.

The Riles (Ryles) family appear to have lived at Little Common for at least a hundred years. In 1637 Thomas Riles was fined for encroaching on the Little Common. The Riles Croft is marked on Fairbank's map of 1760. In 1683 Stephen Riles, husbandman, was farming there with his wife, Elizabeth, and their two daughters, Anne and Elizabeth. The farm had a dwelling house, two barns and a stable and appears to have been near to where Woodville is today on Little Common Lane. In 1728 Jonathan Riles was warned by the Ecclesall Manorial Court that he would be fined if he didn't erect a "sufficient gate to the Abbey Lane", no doubt to stop his animals from straying.

The Downes family owned land at Little Common in 1725 and possibly before that time. They owned land on either side of Little Common Lane which included the Riles Croft. In the Ecclesall Enclosure Award, Charles Downes was awarded land at Little Common in respect of Sarah Downes deceased. In 1760 he owned a large parcel of land and property near Whirlow Hall, but when a survey of the area was carried out in 1807, their Whirlow lands and farms had passed into new ownership.

After the Ecclesall Enclosure Award of 1788, the tenants of the Whirlow farms and cottages not only lost their commons and waste ground as the land passed into private ownership, but also the ancient manorial rights that went with them. The right to collect wood, to take gorse, heath and tree loppings for fuel and most importantly the right to pasture their animals on the common, were now denied them. There was one small area of common however that was retained. The inhabitants of all the cottages at Little Common were to have the privilege of fetching water from the well on the Common. They were to approach the well from Bushey Croft Lane (Abbey Lane). The well was situated in front of the Rising Sun near to the old chestnut tree.

THE RISING SUN

At the end of the 18th Century, Sampson Brookshaw, was the landlord of the Rising Sun on Abbey Lane. As we have seen he was also a cutler. Sampson Brookshaw is perhaps better known today as the friend of the wood collier who was burnt to death in his cabin in Ecclesall Woods. So many people have already written about the tragic events of that night in October 1786 when George Yardley died and of the headstone erected by the four men whose names are inscribed upon it, but few have recorded that Sampson Brookshaw Innkeeper, became the landlord of the Rising Sun. In a directory of 1787

The Rising Sun 1956.

45

Sampson Brookshaw is one of four men who lived at Little Common who are recorded as making pocket knives. These men, Sampson Brookshaw, Joseph Hallam, Abraham Revel and William Abel, all served their apprenticeship, were Freemen of the Cutlers' Company and had been given their own trade mark.

The knives they made were known as "Couteaux", the French word for knives. The French cutlers were causing the Sheffield cutlers much concern with their increasing competition. Although their knives were not as sturdy as the Sheffield ones, they were often more elegant and decorative and sometimes featured two blades. Perhaps the Little Common men were copying the French style pocket knife as a way of beating this competition, hence the name, but this is only conjecture.

In Peter Pegge Burnell's rentals and accounts for the Beauchief estate during the period 1778-1813 a Sampson Brookshaw is recorded as tenanting part of the Hudcliffe Wheel, the wheel situated where Beauchief Station is today. After Sampson Brookshaw's death in 1813, William Loukes, also a Freeman of the Cutlers' Company, took over the tenancy. William Loukes married Sarah Brookshaw, Sampson's daughter, and in time followed his father-in-law as landlord of the Rising Sun. I feel they must be the same people — the dates are correct, the wheel was not far down the lane from the Rising Sun, the names are the same — the coincidences are too great for it to be otherwise.

It was customary after the tenants had paid their rents for the landlord to provide a dinner for his tenants. Mr. Pegge Burnell was no exception. He paid Sampson Brookshaw's bill for the rent day "Dinner Bill at Brookshaw's

The Cottages, Abbey Lane including Mary Thorpe's shop, circa 1900.

(The Sheffield Post Card Co. Ltd.)

46

The Rising Sun with adjoining cottage, circa 1904. The cottage was pulled down around 1930. (The Sheffield Post Card Co. Ltd.)

February 1806 £1.11.0''. May we assume that the jollifications took place at the Rising Sun?

In August 1808 William and Sarah were obviously beginning to take over the work of the pub, for in the rentals we have "Paid William Loukes for dinner and ale". There were eleven people for dinner at 2/6d per head including Sarah's father, Sampson. The ale they consumed cost 15/-. Mrs. Loukes was paid 2/6d for cooking the dinner! There is also an interesting charge of 7/3d for knives. Had Mr. Pegge Burrell purchased some of Sampson Brookshaw's pocket knives for himself or did he give them to the tenants?

William and Sarah Loukes remained at the Rising Sun for many years. Sarah bore ten children, their eldest boy, Sampson, was named after his grandfather. By 1851 William had retired to Parkhead where he lived with his daughter, Fanny Bramwell. Sarah died in 1851, William in 1852.

After William Loukes retired, James Ellis became the new landlord to be followed by George Thorpe. When George died, his widow Hannah carried on the business. It was not unusual for a woman to run a pub. Grace Barker was landlady of the Wheatsheaf at Parkhead in 1807.

The Thorpes were another family who lived at Little Common for generations. In 1871 Joseph and Mary Thorpe were running a small shop at Abbey Lane. After Joseph died, Mary continued the business where she sold tobacco. Her grand-daughter, the late Mrs. Shipman, told me that Mrs. Thorpe was known to everyone as Granny Thorpe. Before the days of the National Health Service, Granny Thorpe was the equivalent of midwife and nurse called in to help at the momentous occasions of birth and death.

The Rising Sun has obviously been altered and extended many times from the small cottage where it had its beginnings. In 1902 the Inn was put up for sale by the trustees of the late Mitchell-Withers of the Woodlands (Parkhead House), who had owned it. Lot 8 was a freehold public house with adjoining cottage, stable, carriage house, paddock and garden. The ivy-clad cottage was pulled down when the Rising Sun had one of its many alterations. The garden still remains, a pleasant place to sit on a summer's evening, the paddock is now the car park and the stables are today the home of the Castle Mountaineering Club.

THE COTTAGES, ABBEY LANE

The main occupations listed in the census returns for the middle of the 19th Century of the people of Abbey Lane and Little Common are grinders, mostly for scythes and file smiths. The Garfitts and later the Mountfords had their scythe works at Wellfield House. The Hallams followed by the Cox's had their works on Little Common Lane and there was the Hudcliffe grinding wheel at Beauchief. This area must have produced a pool of skilled men as sons followed fathers into the trade.

The cutlers lived on Little Common Lane and in a group of cottages opposite to Wellfield House on Abbey Lane. Some of these cottages are marked on the map of 1725. They were home to the pocket knife cutlers of the 18th Century and it was for these dwellings that the well was retained on the common in 1788. In 1902 these cottages were put up for sale by the trustees of the late Mitchell-Withers and were in the same sale as that of the Rising Sun. Lot 7 was recorded as nine freehold cottages with gardens and conveniences, but the cottages were now tenanted by people with a much wider range of occupations, for many of the grinders had moved on.

During the middle of the 20th Century, certain forward thinking people were beginning to realise that it wasn't always necessary to demolish old buildings which no longer met health requirements. It was possible not only to retain our heritage but also to preserve and restore the buildings to meet the required standards of modern living.

Professor Forster, then local chairman of the Council for the Preservation of Rural England, wrote to the Sheffield newspapers in July 1939 putting forward a plea that the charming old houses which adorn the upper portion of Abbey Lane should not be served with a demolition order, similar to the one put on a group of cottages at Parkhead. Sadly, although the Abbey Lane cottages survived for at least another twenty years, they were ultimately pulled down.

The four cottages, set well back from the road, although not nearly as old as the demolished cottages, still survive and were re-roofed in 1989. I think it is possible that the cottages, originally owned by John Mitchell-Withers, were built by him at the time he built the Woodlands (Parkhead House) around 1864, to house the staff needed to run it.

In 1902 one of these cottages was let to Sheffield Corporation for use as a police station. There were a number of cottages allocated in the area for policemen. Matthew Bruce, police officer, lived at the Hoyle Houses, Ringinglow Road in 1871. The cottage at the corner of Trap Lane and Ringinglow Road was a police house in 1900 and one of the cottages on Bents Road was also used as a police house. The local bobby was a familiar sight before the Second World War.

A great deal of new building started in Ecclesall and Whirlow in the late 1920's and 1930's as land was released for building. In Kelly's directory for 1926 there are just four householders on the wood side of Abbey Lane, by 1933 this had increased to twenty-three. As the century progressed and prosperity increased more development took place, the proximity of Ecclesall Woods making it an attractive and desirable place in which to live.

ECCLESALL WOODS

At the time of the Domesday Book, vast tracts of Hallamshire were covered with forest of which Ecclesall Woods were a part. They were renowned for their beautiful trees, hazels, chestnuts and venerable oaks. In the 14th Century they were probably a deer park.

In 1587 the Earl of Shrewsbury claimed that he, his father and grandfather, ''used sett and placed crossbows to kill the deer in Ecclesall Woods and to hunt at all times when it pleased them''.

As the centuries unfolded these great woodlands, once the sporting ground of the nobility were to provide not only pasturage, but wood for building and for charcoal, bark for tanning and work too for some of the Whirlow men.

In early times the woods were sufficiently free of underwood to be pasturable, pigs were driven there to feed on acorns and beechmast. By the 17th Century fenced areas of the woodlands were leased to local farmers for pasturage. The rates for gist as it is called were charged for a stipulated time, usually on a monthly or weekly basis. John Oates of Whirlow was paying rent for herbage in 1627 and in 1703 Anthony Offerton paid 4/- to graze his mare for a month. In 1709 John Riles of Little Common, Henry Fowler and John Dungworth of Whirlow Lane and Joshua Storke of Alms Hill Farm also took advantage of this facility. Cow Lane, an ancient lane running from Abbey Lane into Ecclesall Woods, is marked on Gelley's map of 1725. It was probably the access to the woods the farmers would use to take their animals to graze, which might also account for the name.

By 1587 the woods had been converted into ''spring woods'' when they were farmed for their wood. The trees were coppiced in rotation every fifteen to twenty years, the bark stripped in the previous year for use in the tanning industry. Certain trees were left to grow to maturity and were felled at intervals of sixty to eighty years. The tree roots were ''stubbed up'' to be converted into charcoal. Areas of cleared woodland are often called ''stubbings''. There are fields at Whirlow adjacent to the wood called Stubbings and Stubbings Bottom. There was a cottage near Whirlow Mill at Whirlow Bridge called Stubbins Cottage.

In 1677 Thomas Offerton was paid £1 for loading great timber from the wood. It had taken four men and four days to grub out the roots of the timber.

In 1730 John Dungworth of Whirlow Hall received payment from Mr. Battie, John Bright's steward, for laying and hedging in Ecclesall Woods. It had required 300 sharpened stakes for which he was paid 4/-. The local men that he had employed to carry out the work were paid 1/- per day. In 1751 John Dungworth was paid a salary of £2.10s.0d per annum for fencing and generally looking after the wood. David Glossop was to receive the same salary for the same job twenty years later! The days of substantial wage increases were still to come.

The Woods were divided up into sections and named. This made for easier management. Wood was in great demand for charcoal and white coal, that is cord-wood dried in a kiln, not charred into charcoal. Wood was used in virtually every facet of everyday life. It was a valuable commodity.

In 1718 when Henry Bright's monetary position was becoming acute, he leased the timber from a parcel of woodland near the Hall to John Rotherham, a notable lead smelter. The lease for four years laid down certain conditions. He was to have the right to stubble, chop and dray, that is cart away, the wood with the provision that the carriers must keep Fenney Lane in good repair and fill up any holes they made with earth.

The ring of the woodsman's axe was not the only sound of industry in the woods. Charcoal had been made there for hundreds of years, alder, oak, beech and hazel trees were all used in its manufacture. Here they grew in profusion. Charcoal was used in enormous quantities by the lead and iron industries in Sheffield. The charcoal burners lived in the wood, whilst the process of converting the timber into charcoal took place.

Lead smelting was also carried out in the wood. In the early 17th Century, lead was smelted in an ore-hearth, the process using white coal. The smelt mills were sited on streams, and some remains can still be seen in Ecclesall Woods.

During the 19th Century, apart from recurring felling and sale of timber, the woodland returned to something of its former forest state. G. R. Fraser reflecting on his youth in the 1850's wrote: "Ecclesall Woods with its fine old trees and lusty bracken seemed to us a patch of the primeval wilderness. We were fond of two enormous hollow oaks which we discovered on the road to Ecclesall Woods each of which was roomy enough to comfortably hold ten for lunch or tea''.

In the 1980's the wood cutters returned to Ecclesall Woods. The Ecclesall Wood Saw Mill off Abbey Lane was opened to deal with surplus timber felled by the Sheffield City Recreation Department. The wood is cut up and used for fencing, picnic tables, stakes, etc. So once again the woods have found work for a new generation of men.

Ecclesall Wood Saw Mill 1987.

The survival of these woodlands so near to a major city is indeed remarkable. For generations historic woodlands have been under threat, in other areas many have been eroded away succumbing to advancing agriculture and building programmes.

For over 600 years Ecclesall Woods belonged to the Lord of the Manor of Ecclesall. In 1927 they were sold. Due to the foresight of the Sheffield City Council and the generosity of Alderman Graves and the Town Trustees they were purchased for the City of Sheffield for £45,000.

CHAPTER SEVEN

Ecclesall Road South...
The Whirlow Road

SURPRISINGLY Ecclesall Road South, the most important road today in Whirlow, was not built until the Turnpike Act of May 1811 authorised the building of a new road from Banner Cross to Fox House. In 1812 a further Act, setting out in detail the terms for building it, was passed.

The Duke of Devonshire, after many frustrations, had eventually succeeded in his attempt to have a main highway running from Derbyshire through Whirlow to Banner Cross and on to Sheffield; this was a more direct route than the old enclosure road.

Turnpike roads, although authorised by Parliament, were usually financed by independent Turnpike Trusts, which became responsible for certain portions of road; in return tolls could be levied to defray some of the costs.

Although certain worthy gentlemen contributed to the cost of building this new road, including £50 from John Dungworth, the main burden of expense fell on the Duke of Devonshire.

This road, to be called the Whirlow Road, cut both the Hollis Estate and Whirlow into two parts, taking a good deal of land from some of the farms in the process. John Lee was paid £5.5.0d for land he lost near Little Common Lane. For some time afterwards records were to describe areas in Whirlow as north or south of the turnpike. The building of this road must have caused great upheaval in the area as it cut through completely virgin land to join up at Parkhead with Ecclesall Wood Road. This old enclosure road ran northwards from Abbey Lane to Parkhead and over Broad Oak Green to the Manchester Turnpike (Ringinglow Road). With the making of the new turnpike it would be diverted as part of it became the present Ecclesall Road South and

Ecclesall Road South looking from Parkhead towards Whirlow, circa 1905.

Bents Road. Until this time there had been no direct route from Parkhead to Whirlow Bridge.

The enormous amount of work required to build a new road of these proportions without the assistance of mechanised labour is hard to envisage. The surface was made of limestone. In winter, churned up by horses and waggons it became a sea of mud and in summer a mass of white dust. Even as late as the 20th Century, Walter Clarke of Whirlow Farm was employed in the summer to water the road to keep down the dust.

The building of the Turnpike Road provided additional work for the Whirlow men; both William and Joshua Dungworth were paid for carting stone from the quarries. It was broken into pieces the size of a fist, spread on the road and the traffic would then compress it into a cohesive mass. Water troughs were set at the roadside for the horses at a cost of 4/6d each.

An old date stone of 1816 at Whirlow Bridge gave some indication of when this stretch of the road was completed although it was some years later before the whole turnpike was finished.

The building of the Turnpike Road, together with the new prosperity in Sheffield, was to mark the beginning of a new era in Whirlow. Until this time Whirlow Hall had been the largest farm and the farmers were mostly tenants of Earl Fitzwilliam and the Hollis Trust.

By the middle of the 19th Century Sheffield had become a manufacturing town of some importance and the cutlery trade was world famous. The introduction of steam power, the development of the railways, together with the proximity of coal and the invention of crucible steel by Huntsman, had resulted in the rise of the great steel firms of the east-end of the town which were becoming the power houses of Sheffield industry.

These factories were not only producing fine products but also great quantities of smoke which, together with the prevailing westerly wind, produced air pollution on a considerable scale. The wealthier citizens found it desirable to leave their houses in the centre and east end of the town and to build new and imposing properties on the western outskirts. This not only provided a cleaner environment, but also an opportunity to build large houses on a scale indicative of their wealth and position. The pleasant environs of Whirlow were ideally suited to fulfil their needs and aspirations.

WHIRLOW GRANGE

The first of the large houses to be built on the new stretch of road between Parkhead and Whirlow Bridge was Whirlow Cottage, today the Sheffield Diocesan Conference Centre. In 1833 Henry Waterfall, an attorney, purchased a plot of land near Whirlow Bridge from Earl Fitzwilliam. He asked William Flockton, the notable Sheffield architect to submit plans for the new house. Henry and his wife, Anne, moved into their new home in 1840.

By 1873 Whirlow Cottage had been renamed Whirlow Grange, a more befitting name for a house of these proportions. A conservatory opened from

Whirlow Grange.

the dining room, a croquet lawn and bowling green had been made in the garden together with a kitchen garden and orchard. In 1898 a ballroom was added. It had become fashionable to have ballrooms in the grander houses. There had been an upsurge in improvements and additions to the Whirlow mansions at this time as their owners became more prosperous and, with a plentiful supply of domestic servants, entertaining and hospitality in Whirlow appears to have reached new heights.

For the girls in rural areas there was very little opportunity of finding work except in domestic service. The building of these houses provided them with work but the pay was minimal. Without these willing hands, however, it would have been impossible to run these large establishments. The majority of the indoor servants were women and girls, with the odd man to carry the coal; fireplaces in all the main rooms as well as the nurseries and bedrooms required frequent replenishment.

The great contrast in life-style between the old tenant farming families of Whirlow and the owners of the grand houses that were being built on the Whirlow Road, was to become increasingly apparent as the 19th Century progressed.

For the Victorian lady of the large house, life, apart from supervision of her household, was a pleasant round of social duties, a very different world from that of the farmer's wife, where water had often to be carried from the well and where there was little time for relaxation. In the summer months it was sometimes necessary for the whole family to work in the fields from early morning to late at night. Rural life at this time basks in a romantic glow, but in reality with none of the mechanisation and conveniences of today, every chore must have taken twice as long and been twice as arduous.

For the wealthy there was a carriage or in winter time a sleigh. Sleighs were often used in the snow, which was not removed from the roads but left to become compacted. In these conditions they were much easier for the horses to pull than wheeled vehicles. Mrs. Unwin who lived at Thrift House in the early part of the 20th Century used to be taken to Hill Top (Bents Green) in a horse drawn sleigh. It is recorded that there were great snow storms in Whirlow in 1814 and 1880, the lanes filled in with snow from one hedge to another. It is not surprising that the gap in life-style between the two groups of people living in Whirlow must have seemed enormous.

The next major property to be built on the Whirlow Road was Whirlow House.

WHIRLOW HOUSE

Frederick Wilson, a solicitor, built Whirlow House on land adjacent to Whirlow Cottage (Grange) in 1841. The grounds were extensive: when Whirlow House was sold in 1935, they covered an area of over 14 acres, stretching from Rose Cottage at Whirlow Green down to Ecclesall Road South. In 1848 a new breakfast room was added and in 1849 the house was purchased

Whirlow House and Grounds, circa 1912. Demolished 1977.

by Henry Furniss, a steel manufacturer. He lived there with his wife Ann, a cook, housemaid and a waiting maid.

By 1881 James Fawcett, his wife Lily and their five children had moved in to Whirlow House. For prosperous upper middle class families in Victorian England living-in domestic servants were a necessity; they were also a measure of a family's status. James had engaged a cook, two housemaids, a nurse and, to further his children's education, a German governess. A groom to look after the horses lived above the stables.

The house was subsequently sold to Bernard Firth of the steel manufacturers Thomas Firth and in 1902 it was purchased by Edgar Allen.

Edgar Allen, of Edgar Allen, Sheffield, manufacturers and shipping merchants, was a prosperous and influential man; he was also a philanthropic one. In 1909 the Prince and Princess of Wales opened the Edgar Allen Library at the new University of Sheffield. On this occasion Edgar Allen gave £5,000 to both the Sheffield Infirmary and the Royal Hospital. In 1911 the Edgar Allen Institute opened in Gell Street to give free medical treatment to the "wage-earning classes". Edgar Allen not only paid for all the equipment of the Institute but also its maintenance for three years. As a result of his many interests and social standing he required a residence that would reflect his position and at Whirlow House he was able to live in some style.

Over the years many alterations to the house and grounds had taken place. There were extensive outbuildings; an engine house had been constructed for the manufacture of electric light, there was a motor house too for the latest mechanical marvel, the automobile. The stables faced on to a cobbled courtyard behind the house. There was stabling for five horses, a harness and groom's room on the ground floor with a coachman's flat above.

The grounds were a delight, large and spacious they had all the attributes of a small estate. There were two ornamental ponds, a natural spring flowed through a small grotto, there was a Japanese garden and a rock garden. Near to the stables were the potting and tool sheds, greenhouses and a forcing house, but perhaps from a gardener's point of view the most exciting of all were an orchid house and a banana house. Edgar Allen took great pleasure in escorting his dinner guests to pick their own bananas for dessert; they were much appreciated by those who had never tasted fresh fruit of such perfection before!

After Edgar Allen's death, the house was sold in 1915 to Edward Dixon from Whirlow Croft. The family remained at Whirlow House until 1935 when it was offered for auction. Whirlow House was purchased by Sheffield Corporation in 1938 and later used by the Ministry of Pensions, and in 1951 by the Ministry of National Insurance. By the 1970's although the house had been maintained, the lovely gardens had become a wilderness. The conservatories, orchid and banana houses, of which Edgar Allen had been so proud, were derelict and falling down, their glass broken and saplings growing through the windows. The ornamental ponds had been filled in, the Japanese Gardens and tennis court were no more and traces of the grotto could just be found in the undergrowth.

Part of the grounds were being used as playing fields by the Sheffield Works Department's Sports and Social Club.

Sadly the house, once the home of some of Sheffield's most influential citizens was demolished in 1977. The courtyard stable block remained for a time, before it too was pulled down.

SCRAT HOUSES

Near the deep bend in the road at 480-482 Ecclesall Road South were three old stone cottages, two of them faced the road, the other was at the back. All that remains today to mark where they once stood is a portion of wall, part of the front of the cottages.

The cottages were called Scrat Houses. The "scrat" was a wild shaggy wood-sprite. When the cottages were built they were surrounded by trees; this is probably how they got their name. The street lamp in the photograph replaced an old ornate gas lamp powered by sewer gas which was lit day and night.

The cottages were built by William Hallam on land leased from Earl Fitzwilliam. William was a cutler and in 1833 was making penknives at Little Common. I think he built the Scrat Houses after the Turnpike was pushed through Whirlow to Whirlow bridge, because they followed the line of the new road.

By 1841 William was living in the largest cottage with his wife Hannah and his mother, Ann. He leased the two other cottages to a plasterer and his family and to a young agricultural labourer, Thomas Reeve, his wife Harriet, and their baby son, George. Over the years the Scrat Houses were to become home to many people. In 1926 Francis Rowland Walker, taking up employment in Whirlow, brought his family over from Barnsley to live in the double fronted

Scrat Houses, February 1969. Now empty, the windows boarded up prior to demolition.

cottage. His young son, Rowland, was fascinated by the large houses in the neighbourhood and by the influential men who lived in them. He determined that one day he too would make his mark on the city of Sheffield. In October 1987 Rowland Walker, OBE, became the Master of the Company of Cutlers in Hallamshire, not only fulfilling his own ambitions but continuing in a line of Whirlow men to hold that office.

Possibly because the cottages were on a difficult bend in the road, it was decided to demolish the Scrat Houses and the photograph shows the empty cottages in February 1969 prior to demolition.

ST. ANN'S

The area around Whirlow Croft, Broomcroft, Parkhead House and part of Abbey Lane was known in the middle of the 19th Century as St. Ann's. I do not know why. The house sitting between Abbey Lane and Ecclesall Road South is known as St. Ann's. Built, according to the date stone, in 1855, it has been enlarged and altered many times. Over the years the grounds have been reduced as the land was sold for building. There was a St. Ann's Hotel too.

In 1851 John Wilson, a tailor, was living near Whirlow Croft with his wife, Mary, their nine children and his brother, Samuel, a shoe-maker. By 1861 his dwelling had become known as the St. Ann's Hotel and John had become a publican. Possibly as a result of the increase in travellers on the Whirlow Road (Ecclesall Road South) he had found a way of augmenting his income. When the next census was taken in 1871 John and his family had left. Samuel Wilson had moved to Broad Oak and there is no further mention of the St. Ann's Hotel in the records.

In 1871 William Clarke was living at Woodview, St. Ann's. He is recorded as being a grocer and general dealer. He was the son of Joseph Clarke of Whirlow Green. He had married Hezia Johnson in December 1853 and for the early part of their married life they lived at Whirlow Green where their three daughters were born. William worked on the farm.

In the middle of the 19th Century there were very few shops in the area. John and Elizabeth Hancock sold groceries at Parkhead. John Hill had a shop at Hilltop (Bents Green) and Mary Thorpe sold tobacco at Little Common. With his family increasing steadily every two years, William possibly saw the opportunity of a more profitable way of earning his living and looking after his growing family. He opened his shop some time between 1861 and 1871, selling groceries, ironmongery, hardware and lamps. He was still running the shop in 1895, but by 1905 Woodview had become a private residence.

The building of the large houses in Whirlow continued as the 19th Century progressed. In 1864 a young and prominent Sheffield architect, John Mitchell-Withers, designed a large and imposing residence on a parcel of land bordering Ecclesall Road South, Little Common Lane and Abbey Lane. It was to be the first of three houses that he and later his son were to design on Ecclesall Road

Parkhead House. Formerly known as The Woodlands.

South. But this house was for his own occupation and having built it, he lived there for the rest of his life.

THE WOODLANDS — PARKHEAD HOUSE

The house that Mitchell-Withers designed for himself was called The Woodlands. It was a house of fine proportions, the first floor approached by an imposing stone staircase with an oak and iron balustrade. The dining room was reputed to have been panelled with 16th Century oak taken from the long gallery of the old Manor House in Sheffield.

There were kitchen gardens and orchards, stables and loose-boxes, a carriage house, harness room and all the other essential requirements of a Victorian gentlemen's residence. Set in parkland, the house was approached from Ecclesall Road South and another drive led down to the stables and out into Abbey Lane. The grounds were landscaped with a great many trees. A cook, parlour maid, nurse and housemaid were employed to see to the running of the house. A gardener and coachman looked after the garden and stables.

John moved into The Woodlands in 1864-65. He was only 28 at the time. By 1871 he and Lise, his wife, had three children. John, the eldest, was to follow in his father's footsteps and become a respected architect. Sadly John Mitchell-Withers Senior was to die at an early age and in June 1898, the house was sold to Robert Hadfield, the managing director of Hadfields with vast works in Attercliffe and Tinsley. He embarked on substantial alterations, adding a two storey block comprising billiard room, library, two further bedrooms and a bathroom. The Woodlands too acquired a new name, Parkhead House.

Robert Hadfield was a J.P. He became Master of the Cutlers' Company in Hallamshire in 1899 and he was a Freeman of the City of London. In 1908 he was knighted. Parkhead House remained one of the family homes for forty years.

For some time Sheffield Corporation had been looking for a house which could be used for Judges' lodgings when the Assize Courts opened in Sheffield. When Parkhead House was put on the market in November 1938 it seemed ideal for this purpose. It was duly purchased for £6,750 in 1939 but probably as a result of the Second World War these plans were shelved and in 1948 it was adapted and opened as a house for thirty-five elderly men.

Over the years the grounds surrounding the house became reduced as parcels of land were sold for building. At some stage the 16th Century oak from Sheffield Manor was removed, the fine fireplaces were blocked up, but glimpses of its past grandeur remained.

The Dining Room of Parkhead House, circa 1924, then the home of Sir Robert Hadfield.
(Sheffield City Libraries)

In 1988 Parkhead House became surplus to requirements. The elderly gentlemen moved out and it was put up for auction. With over four acres of land and situated in a prime position, it was a very desirable piece of real estate and it was sold in June 1989 for £1.2 million.

BROOMCROFT

In 1883 David Davy of Davy Brothers, the engineers and boiler makers, purchased a plot of land from Richard Bayley who was then living at Whirlow Grange. The land bordering Whirlow Lane and Ecclesall Road South had wonderful views looking over towards Ecclesall Wood and Beauchief to the hills beyond. David Davy asked Mitchell-Withers to design a house for him. He called it Broomcroft.

The house, together with extensive outbuildings, carriage house and stables, tennis courts, croquet lawns and a tea house, was approached through a

Top: Broomcroft. Built for David Davy, it was first occupied in 1887.

Centre: The Tea House, Broomcroft. Note the windows in the roof for additional light.

Left: The Terrace Walk in the gardens of Broomcroft.

61

handsome two storey entrance lodge. The grounds also featured a terrace walk, a paddock for the horses, a large kitchen garden with vinery and glass houses. Stone built, the house was an imposing and substantial residence. In 1892 a two storey addition of servants' hall and nursery was added.

The main hall was impressive. The first floor approached by an oak staircase was backed by very fine stained glass windows depicting the four seasons. They were a series of twelve beautiful leaded windows in groups of four, featuring flowers, seasonal activities and the story of Robin Hood. The house contained many fine chimney pieces, perhaps the finest being in the dining room; made of Ashford Marble, with an oak covered mantle, the interior was fitted with brilliant blue cornflower tiles by William de Morgan, a famous artist whose tiles were used in many great Victorian houses.

David Davy died and in 1923 Broomcroft was sold. In 1928 Ecclesall Road South was widened and houses were beginning to edge their way from Parkhead towards Broomcroft. Perhaps it was at this time that some of the land was sold, for the entrance lodge was pulled down, two cottages in the grounds were demolished and the entrance drive then opposite to St. Ann's was moved.

The house remained a private residence until it was given to the City of Sheffield by George Jowitt in 1953. It was adapted as a home for the elderly and continued to be used by the local authority for this purpose until 1988. Broomcroft, together with its land, now reduced to 3½ acres from over 10 acres in 1923, was auctioned in April 1989 and sold for £1.4 million.

WHIRLOW — CLIFFORD HOUSE

It is quite remarkable how many of the houses and farms built in Whirlow before the 20th Century have Whirlow as part of their name. It is quite probable, with the increase in urban development and the numbering of houses, that house names after this time were no longer a necessity. In 1894 when Denys Hague, a colliery owner, moved into his new home, names were all important, particularly for a house of some eminence. He called his new home Whirlow; his address Whirlow at Whirlow, Nr. Sheffield, was certainly imposing. Whirlow was designed by John Mitchell-Withers Junior who as a boy had lived next door at the Woodlands (Parkhead House).

The parkland of the house stretched down to Abbey Lane and its westerly boundary met the old footpath which ran from Ecclesall Road South to Abbey Lane.

By 1897 Charles Clifford had made Whirlow his home. He was the Chairman of the *Sheffield Telegraph* and *Star*, but his name is probably better known today as one of the benefactors of the Charles Clifford Dental Hospital. In 1925 Charles Clifford was knighted and in February 1935 he presented Broombank, a house on Glossop Road, to the University of Sheffield to be used as a dental hospital. The dental hospital that bears his name is today situated off Whitham Road. Lady Clifford remained at Whirlow after Sir Charles died in 1936.

Children in Croft Lane with Whirlow Court in the background, circa 1905.

There was some suggestion that during the Second World War the house would be acquired by the Government for the Aircraft Production Department, but that wasn't to be. The estate was purchased by the United Steel Co. Ltd. in 1942 and it was after this time that the house changed its name from Whirlow to Clifford House, possibly to avoid confusion with other similarly named houses in the area.

The parkland no longer borders Abbey Lane for in 1971/2 the Whirlowdale Park estate was built on part of this land.

WHIRLOW COURT

Whirlow Court, for a time during the latter part of the 20th Century the Lord Mayor of Sheffield's official residence, became one of the city's most prestigious addresses; it was built by one of Sheffield's most prestigious families — the Fawcetts.

James Dixon Fawcett, part owner of the silverware and cutlery firm of James Dixon and Sons Limited, was the grandson of James Dixon, the founder of the firm. His mother, Ann, married William Fawcett who in 1855/56 was Mayor of Sheffield. James and Lily Fawcett built Whirlow Court in the early 1880's; in order to supervise the building of their new house they moved with their family from Broom Hall to Whirlow House, just across the road from their future home.

The laying of the foundation stone was an occasion for some ceremony. James Fawcett's small daughter, Madge laid the stone with a silver trowel and a box containing a copy of the local Sheffield newspaper, together with some current coins of the realm, was buried in the foundations.

The Fawcetts moved into their substantial and imposing home; the parkland and gardens covered many acres, Whirlowdale Road, Whirlow Court Road and

Whirlow Grove were still in the future. Their land stretched down to Abbey Lane and Ecclesall Woods and a considerable way in both directions along Ecclesall Road South.

James and Lily had six children — five sons, Ernest, Alfred, Percy, Noel and Wortley, and Madge, their only daughter. With their large house and grounds it was necessary to employ a staff of twelve to look after the family and to help run the establishment. When James Fawcett died in 1900 his son Alfred, now a solicitor, lived at Whirlow Court.

The people living in the large houses at Whirlow found it a pleasant area in which to live. As with the farming families of the previous century, the inhabitants of the neighbouring houses were often related and they enjoyed having their families near at hand. The young people living in these substantial houses would have every opportunity to meet their contemporaries at the social gatherings which took place in them.

Alfred Fawcett married a daughter of Major William Greaves Blake of Mylnhurst on Button Hill. Alfred's brother, Percy, married the daughter of Frederick Charles Wild and by 1905 the Wilds had moved into Whirlow Court, their son-in-law's former home. Frederick Wild, a magistrate and prominent businessman, had been Master Cutler in 1898/99. He remained at Whirlow Court until he died in January 1920.

Alfred Fawcett purchased Standhills on Long Line in Dore. Standhills was renowned for its game and fine shooting, a pastime greatly enjoyed by Edwardian gentlemen and two lakes in the grounds provided excellent coarse fishing. Alfred's brother, Percy, wishing to be near the family, built Whirlow Brook near Whirlow Bridge. When Whirlow Croft came up for sale in 1915 Francis Wild, Frederick's son and Percy's brother-in-law, decided to buy it, so for a time, the Wild family were to live in close proximity to one another.

After Frederick's Wild's death in 1920, Whirlow Court was sold to Arthur Davy, the Sheffield grocer. Davys were bakers and provision merchants of renown. Their premises in Fargate also contained the Victoria Café which was not only a popular venue for meeting friends, but a regular lunch-time haunt for city businessmen.

Arthur Davy died in 1946 sitting in his bedroom after a busy but happy day felling trees in his garden.

Whirlow Court came up for sale again in March 1946. By this time the grounds, although still large, were not as extensive as they had once been. Whirlowdale Road had been cut through from Millhouses to Whirlow in the mid 1920's. According to the Sheffield Year Book and Record of 1923, the costs of building the road had risen and the Council had found it necessary to revise their original estimate and increase it to £50,166, a problem most town Councils must be familiar with. One wonders how much the road would cost to build today. Whirlow Court Road named after the house and Whirlow Grove were built on original Whirlow Court land. The first houses were occupied around 1930, but it was 1934 before the road was finally adopted.

Although reduced in size, the grounds of Whirlow Court still covered over nine acres. They were very beautiful. Photographs of the time show great quantities of rose bushes and wonderful herbaceous borders spilling over with a profusion of flowers. There were clipped yews, a rock garden and a stream flowed through small pools into a boating lake. The parkland swept down to a long frontage bordering Whirlowdale Road and the views from the house over the woods to the moors were extensive.

The Batchelors were the last family to live in Whirlow Court as a family home, for its days as a private residence were numbered. Lt. Colonel Maurice Batchelor, J.P., was the Chairman of Batchelors Peas. In 1954 Whirlow Court was sold to Sheffield Corporation. The Sheffield Assize Courts were due to open in 1955 and it was to become lodgings for visiting Judges.

Over the years more land has been used for development. Whirlowdale Close with its approach from Whirlowdale Road carved into the parkland and in 1984 the *Sheffield Telegraph* reported that due to cut backs in financial support, the Sheffield City Council were selling some of the land for private housing. The new road, Whirlowdale Rise, was built, not without protest from local residents, on part of the ornamental gardens and croquet lawn of Whirlow Court.

Whirlow Court has seen many notable people pass through its portals, including Princess Anne when she visited Whirlow in 1980. William Fawcett could hardly have imagined that the house built by his son, James, would become in the future the official residence of the Lord Mayor of Sheffield, the office that he had held in 1855.

HOLLIS HOSPITAL

On Ecclesall Road South, near to Whirlow Bridge, there is a group of buildings approached by a long drive — it is known as Hollis Hospital.

Thomas Hollis, a dissenter, was born in Rotherham in 1634. In 1648 he was apprenticed to his uncle, John Ramsker, a Sheffield cutler. He left Sheffield during his apprenticeship to manage his uncle's business in London. Thomas was a religious and kindly man, he showed great interest in the poor and in the education of the young. He was not only industrious but benevolent and in 1704 set up a Trust to endow a building near Snig Hill in Sheffield, which he converted into sixteen dwellings for the care of elderly widows whose husbands had been in the cutlery and allied trades. After he died in 1718, his son, another Thomas, together with other members of the Hollis family, added to the endowment. In 1726 he purchased the Whirlow Hall estate which included Whirlow Mill and 146 acres of land. These lands and properties, now in the hands of tenant farmers, were to be supervised by the Trustees of the Hollis Trust.

In 1903 the land where Hollis Hospital was situated was required for road improvements. It was decided to move away from the city to the open countryside at Whirlow and to build a new hospital on land the Trust owned near Whirlow Bridge. In this delightful setting there are now self-catering flatlets within Hollis Hospital where single or widowed ladies are still cared for by the Trust, started so long ago by Thomas Hollis.

WHIRLOW MILL

Streams have always been a valuable resource but in early times they were an essential part of everyday living, often supplying the drinking water for man and beast and if they were suitable, a source of power. The position of the mill was determined by the gradient of the stream. Whirlow was fortunate that the Lymbrook flowing down from the high moors above Ringinglow to Whirlow Bridge was a potential source of water power.

The mill at Whirlow, rebuilt in 1734, was originally built for grinding corn, the miller like the blacksmith and wheelwright being an essential part of the farming community. The Whirlow tenants would be expected to patronise the landlord's mill, by taking their grain to the miller for grinding.

Many of the millstones used for grinding were made in Derbyshire, the millstone grit was ideal for the purpose. They can still be seen lying on the moors above Hathersage and Grindleford; a pair of stones for Whirlow Mill cost £6.10s.0d when they were purchased in 1734, a considerable sum of money in those days.

Although the water corn mill at Whirlow Bridge may have been in use before 1586, ratification of John Bright's ownership was given in a law suit of that time, which recorded that the wheel which stood on the Lymbrook was his own property. From that time until it was sold in 1935, the Whirlow wheel remained part of the Whirlow Hall Estate.

There are some fascinating letters written by the Trustees of the Hollis Trust to Timothy Hollis, grandson of Thomas, during the middle of the 18th Century. Mainly they kept him abreast of the happenings and business of the

The remains of Whirlow Mill.

Trust which was wide-spread but occasionally there were details in the letters about Whirlow and the Trust's property there which mainly refer to Whirlow Mill. The Hollis Trust experienced many problems with the mill after it came into their possession in 1726 not only with the early tenants, who appear to have been a difficult and untrustworthy group of people, but also in the sheer expense of keeping the mill running and in working order.

One of their early tenants Joseph Nicholls was mentioned in numerous letters; although the Trust had been given good references as to his carefulness and diligence there were to be many problems during his seven years at the mill.

In 1753 the north wall bulged, concern was felt that it had become so dangerous that it would be a hazardous job to replace it. Their fears were justified for "it fell and wounded three persons, one dangerously, but fortunately missed the guts of the mill. It is now rebuilt".

Joseph had certainly been unfortunate. He appears to have spent money on the mill, but in 1756 we hear that the millstones had broken and the mill had lain idle for nine months. Six of his horses had died during the summer and obviously very discouraged, he had begun to sell off the remainder of his hay, his animals and his manure: manure was a valuable commodity. To the distress of the Trust he broke down some fences and absconded in the night, no doubt without paying the rent.

Great relief was expressed when John Marsden, a baker "of very good and visible substance", took over the tenancy in 1757. Unfortunately their faith in him was not rewarded for in a letter of 25th March 1767 Samuel Shore writing to Timothy Hollis in London mentions that John Marsden was not only in arrears, but was last year committed to York "and took his tryal there for an assalt on a woman, and tho' he was acquitted it was attended with some expense and his mother thereby disabled from paying the rent". One can imagine the displeasure this must have caused the upright Mr. Shore.

The problems with the Marsden family were not over, John Marsden died and his family retained the tenancy until the expiration of the lease in 1778. The Trustees had difficulty in regaining possession of the mill for in spite of several visits by the bailiffs "she (there is some difficulty in ascertaining whether 'she' was John's mother or his widow) concealed herself for several weeks to avoid being served with possession". The Trust apparently overcame these problems for the tenancy passed to Alice Marsden's son-in-law, John Swinden, who proved to be "an awkward troublesome person".

The Trustees frequently mention the losses they incurred, the burden and expense of the mill giving the landlords no return on their money. Possibly for these reasons it was decided to install a grinding wheel and to build a new dam. In 1802 the corn mill changed its status: saws and later scythes were manufactured there.

In 1755 the letters mention the discovery of coal at Whirlow, news which was greeted with great enthusiasm. A coal surveyor was called in, shafts were dug, boreholes made and there were hopes of a future coal mine, but it was not to be. It became evident that the coal was not worth extracting; the costs were too high, so the idea was abandoned and the trial pits filled up with water.

There are several references to weather, a wet Autumn in 1756, an uncommonly wet summer in 1763, severe weather in December 1764 but a more dramatic account of bad weather at Whirlow was given in the *Sheffield and Rotherham Independent* on 13th October 1849. The newspaper stated that on the Saturday and Sunday nights, the rain was so heavy and continuous that Sheffield was "visited by a flood", the worst for many years. The streams running down from the high moors above Whirlow, swollen by the heavy rain, poured into the large reservoir dam, constructed to supply the Whirlow Mill with power to run the grinding wheels. The small weir proved inadequate, several yards of embankment gave way with a "fearful crash" and a large mass of stones was swept down the stream causing flooding at Abbeydale.

By 1935 the mill had become very old and dilapidated and its useful life was over. The building was sold to Sheffield Corporation and parts of it are still used.

If you take part of the Round Walk from Limb Lane down towards Ryecroft Glen and Ecclesall Woods you pass the old mill on the left. Undergrowth conceals the contours, rusty metal and rotting wood are all that remain of the wheel. The lower mill dam was filled in when Ecclesall Road South was straightened, but the upper dam remains for everyone to see, its green waters reflecting the surrounding trees in Whirlow Brook Park.

THE MILL HOUSE — WHIRLOW COTTAGE

The old Mill House was situated near to Whirlow Mill on the Lymbrook. When Thomas Hollis visited the Mill in 1727 he mentions a house and land

The New Mill House, Whirlow Cottage, built in 1853.

with a mill and a little house partly in Derbyshire; as we have seen, in those days, the Limb Brook formed the boundary between Yorkshire and Derbyshire. The little house was called the Stubbins Cottage.

George and Mary Hall were living in the Mill House in 1719. Although George was a miller, he was a farmer too. He owned horses, two of them old, a sow, calves and some sheep. There was also a plough and a harrow for breaking up the clods of earth after ploughing. When George died, he left all his personal estate and worldly goods to Mary, although his brothers, Robert and William, were to receive 1/- each. Amongst his effects were some linen yarn and a wheel, possibly a spinning wheel to spin the wool from his flock of sheep.

With the death of George Hall, Henry Bright required a new tenant. On 4th March 1720 he leased the house near Whirlow Mill to Thomas Grieves.

In 1725 the Hollis Trust, the new owners of the mill and Mill House, let the Mill House, part of which had been newly rebuilt, to Joseph Dewes. He also took on the tenancy of the mill and some land. Repairs to the Mill House were carried out after Thomas Hollis' visit in 1727 and again in 1737 when an allowance of £11.0s.8d was sanctioned by the Trustees. But Joseph was not very good at paying his rent and he caused the Trust much irritation.

In 1795 Benjamin Dewsbury moved into the Mill House, which was becoming very old. It was during his time as tenant that the grinding wheel was installed at the Corn Mill in 1802/3 and the mill became known as the Whirlow Wheel. Goodwin and Barker took over the wheel in 1804, when they began to make saws. Benjamin Dewsbury remained in the Mill House.

In 1850 it was decided to build a new cottage. Mr. Wright, a surveyor, was asked to supply estimates for the new building. In 1853 it was agreed to proceed with the plan and specifications were produced by Mr. Fowler, the Hollis Trust surveyor. The estimate of £110 for building the cottage was accepted. In 1853 a new house was built across the Limb Brook on a new site adjacent to land now occupied by Hollis Hospital with a new name, Whirlow Cottage.

When William Furness took over the tenancy of the Whirlow Wheel to make scythes in 1853, it also included the tenancy of the new Whirlow Cottage. Richard Furness was living there in 1926. When Mrs. Mary Furness left Whirlow Cottage in the 1980's, it brought to an end the long association of the Furness family with the Whirlow Hall Estate.

Whirlow Cottage was put up for auction and sold on 24th September 1986.

WHIRLOW BRIDGE INN

The old curve of the Turnpike road remains at Whirlow Bridge. Once a ford, then a bridge, now a road, it is part of the old route up Fenney Lane to Sheffield. It was here where the two houses stand near Whirlow Brook Park gates that the Whirlow Bridge Inn was situated.

Whirlow Bridge in the early days of motoring.

Originally a Beer House, it was built around 1846. It was an attractive double fronted building, with stabling and outbuildings. There was a field for the horses and a garden on the opposite side of the road near the now filled in lower dam of the Whirlow Wheel. It must have been a pleasant place for travellers to stop. In the 1870's Mr. Furness of Whirlow Hall had difficulties with visitors to the Inn trespassing in the nearby private woods. The wooden gate into the woods was continually being broken down as they scrambled through. In 1874 it was found necessary to build a stone wall in an attempt to keep them out. These same beautiful woods now belong to the City of Sheffield. In 1937 they were purchased and given by the J. G. Graves Trust to the City. The Round Walk, of which they are part, was opened on 30th July 1938.

The Inn was owned by the Hollis Trust and leased in 1852 to Watts & Stone. In 1874 Rawsons Brewery took over the lease. Extensive repairs were carried out, the road in front of the Inn was paved and levelled and the outbuildings enlarged. Boating was allowed on the reservoir dam at the back of the Inn, but in 1880 the landlord was reprimanded for allowing three boats when only two were permitted!

In September 1874 the Trustees of the Hollis Trust entered on one of their periodical inspections of their property at Whirlow. Walking from Beauchief station, after taking the train from Sheffield, they were met at Whirlow Bridge. It must have been quite a walk up the steep hill. Fortunately, business concluded, Mr. Furness hospitably entertained them to lunch.

Henry Tatton writing in the 1920's mentioned that a favourite pastime of the people of Sheffield was to walk along Ecclesall Road to the Whirlow Bridge Inn, take a rest, then proceed down Rye Croft Glen to Abbeydale and back to town. The Inn was also a popular halt for vehicular traffic. Subsequently a group of local worthies conspired to remove the licence from the publican because they felt it lowered the tone of the neighbourhood. They were successful — it became a refreshment house and sold ice cream. The Inn, by now a private residence, was demolished in August 1938.

Whirlow Bridge Inn, circa 1904.

WHIRLOW BROOK

Whirlow Brook is known today by the many thousands of people who visit it every year to walk in the grounds and have a cup of tea in the café or perhaps attend one of the many functions held there, but it was built as a private

Whirlow Brook

residence. Before the boundary changes in 1935 this land was in Derbyshire, but today it is very much a part of Whirlow.

Whirlow Brook was built around 1906 when Mr. and Mrs. Percy Fawcett decided to leave their home, Middlewood Hall, and return to Whirlow to be nearer their family. Their new home was built on land which formed part of the Standhills Estate, owned by Percy's brother, Alfred; the position backed by woods and bordered by the Limb Brook was superb. A private footpath was made through the grounds of Standhills and Whirlow Brook to enable the families to visit one another more easily.

Mr. and Mrs. Fawcett remained at Whirlow Brook until 1920 when they moved to Dore Moor House. Percy's sister, Madge, now married to Mr. Walter Benton Jones, also wishing to return to Whirlow moved into Whirlow Brook.

Mrs. Benton Jones was a very keen horticulturist. Although employing six gardeners to care for the estate, she took a great interest herself in the management and design of the garden. The Royal Horticultural Society was invited to advise on the planting and planning of the extensive grounds. The beautiful gardens she helped to create, with their fine trees and shrubs, rock gardens and lakes, remain today for everyone to enjoy. When Madge, now Lady Benton Jones, died in 1938 it was decided to consecrate a piece of ground in her beloved garden in which to bury her. Unfortunately this was to give unforeseen problems to her family in later years when Whirlow Brook was sold and it was necessary to have a reburial.

In 1946, Sir Walter Benton Jones sold Whirlow Brook with its 39½ acres of land. The Town Trustees, the Graves Charitable Trust and Sheffield Corporation purchased it for £15,000. Whirlow Brook Park was opened to the public by the Lord Mayor in 1951.

WHIRLOW GLEN

Many people will be familiar with the delightful walk that threads its way up the valley of the Limb Brook from Whirlow Bridge to Ringinglow. This part of the wooded Limb valley used to be known as Whirlow Glen or Little Switzerland and was originally part of the Whirlow Hall Estate, marked on the maps as the Bole Hill Plantation. It was later owned by the Hollis Trust who in May 1935 agreed to sell it to Sheffield Corporation.

Passing through these woods you eventually reach the ruins of the Copperas House. John Dunstan in *From Dore to Dore* gives a detailed description of the making of copperas, which was used as a mordant for fixing dyes. Another John, John Thomas, writing in 1830, paints a vivid picture of the making of copperas and the Copperas House.

"Here is a long rambling range of buildings, where-in are made the potent sulphates of copper, zinc and iron. The killing scent of this manufacture is visible in its effects and all around the blades of vegetation shrink up or become black, and even the wooden doors and window sashes of the little homestead which is attached to it, open in the grain and rot inwardly. Yet in this place with the hideous stench of copperas pervading every nook and chamber, lives an aged man, the sole worker of the poison, alone, without even the good company of a dog."

Copperas House 1984.

73

Copperas continued to be made there for another twenty years. In time nature took over this desolate and polluted place so graphically described by John Thomas and returned it to the sylvan spot it is today, with just the old dilapidated ruins to remind us of its once industrial past.

The name Bole Hill is also a reminder that in the past the highest part of the Bole Hill Plantation was used for the smelting of lead. Lead was mined in Derbyshire in Roman times, but it wasn't until 1500 that the lead mining industry began to develop. From medieval times to the late 16th Century bole hearths were used in the smelting of lead and there were bole hills at Totley, Crookes and Whirlow too. A simple bole or furnace, about two feet across and fuelled with wood, was usually situated on the top of hills in order to utilise the strong winds which blew there. The bole hill at Whirlow is approximately 900 feet above sea level, an ideal location.

Lead was later smelted at John Bright's Smelting Mill near Whirlow. In a mortgage of 1621, between Lawrence Hall and John Bright of Whirlow Hall, mention is made of ''2 foothers (a foother is a cartload or a specific weight current at the time) of good pure merchantable peake lead to be delivered to the smelting house''.

In 1703 one of the fields near Whirlow Hall was known as Kiln Hill, a possible indication that white coal (that is small pieces of chopped wood dried in a kiln) used in lead smelting was made here. In November 1718 Henry Bright sold to Mr. Rotherham ''all the white coal that shall be made excepting 10 dozen at 5s. 8d. per dozen''. The Rotherhams of Dronfield were substantial lead merchants who owned a large lead mill near Beauchief.

By 1737 the smelters had adopted the cupola furnace, but by this time, the Brights had left Whirlow Hall and the Hollis Trust who now owned the land turned the slopes of the Bole Hill into a tree plantation.

When the Ecclesall Wastes and Commons were enclosed in 1788 the Commissioners of the Enclosure Act awarded land on the High Moor (the high area of land between Whirlow Hall and Ringinglow Road) to the Hollis Trust. Possibly as a result of the award the Trust decided to embark on the customary stone-walling to fence in their new land. During 1788/89 they also carried out a large programme of stone-wall fencing in the Bole Hill Plantation.

Various people were employed to cart the stone and to build the walls. Henry Watson, a labourer, was employed to level and dig the ground in preparation for building the foundations of these walls. For four days' work he was paid 6/8d. Henry's name crops up again in some accounts for the rebuilding of Castle Dyke, again he was paid for four days' labouring. He was obviously a useful odd job man, probably local, who was called in when needed to carry out a variety of manual jobs. Joshua Osborne from the forge at Hilltop (now the Hammer & Pincers, Bents Green), was paid 3/- in 1789 for iron work on the Bole Hill brow.

There is a record of walling on Ecclesall Common in 1788, no doubt on the newly acquired land received in the Enclosure Award. Mr. Mekinson sent his

74

bill to John Ash of the Hollis Trust. The bill was not only for the work that he had carried out, but also for a man with a horse and cart to clear away the rubbish after the masons had "done walling". For two and a half days' work the man received 10/-, for the carriage of two large stones for the gateway into the new enclosure 4/-. There is also a record for money spent on liquor which was given to the workmen and labourers whilst they were working on the dry stone walls; whether this was a kindly gesture on the part of the employers or part of the contract the records don't reveal.

The walls built by the masons over 200 years ago still stand for the most part, fencing in the Bole Hill Plantation.

In 1791 the Hollis Trust advertised for sale some wood from the Whirlow Wood. The trees to be felled were marked and the wood was sold at the King's Head in Sheffield on 7th June. The King's Head, a posting inn, was well known. It was situated in Change Alley and from there every Monday and Friday at noon Nicholsons' waggon left for York, calling at Doncaster, Ferrybridge and Tadcaster. Mr. Ash paid 2/6d for two days' hire of a room at the King's Head.

In 1821 Mr. Samuel Shore of the Hollis Trust asked the surveyor, Josiah Fairbank, to carry out a survey of the Whirlow Bridge plantation. In July of that year Mr. Fairbank in fine handwriting forwarded his report. Although favourable he had suggestions to make on the future plantings of trees in the plantation. Larch, spruce, oak and ash he felt would thrive in the local soil.

The Hollis Trust used the Whirlow Wood as a resource and as another way of producing income to pay for the running of their hospital and schools. In 1870 there is a note in the Hollis Papers that many trees had died and on 1st October 1874 there is a record that the timber had been sold and £7 had been spent on the planting of young trees.

These woods so carefully managed in earlier centuries, were until 1935 private property. Today they now provide a welcome area for relaxation. They are however a heritage which must be preserved and cared for. We all have a responsibility to see that they remain in good order for future generations to enjoy.

WHIRLOW QUARRY

The quarry gardens at Whinfell were built in the former Whirlow Quarry. Mr. Camm was leasing the quarry from the Hollis Trust in 1851 and in 1863 he was paying rent at £15 per annum. The Trust paid Mr. Camm £5 to oversee the Bole Hill Plantation and for the mole rate. Moles always have been and still are troublesome in this part of Whirlow.

The stone was quarried and taken down to the Turnpike by a system of rails. In November 1869 Mr. Camm filled up part of the quarry and opened up a new area nearer to Fenney Lane. Four men were working here, but by 1870 this had been reduced to three. The Hollis Trust had experienced a few problems with Mr. Camm and he in turn had found the new workings very costly to operate; in 1873 he gave up the lease.

Jonathan Hulley who had been Mr. Camm's foreman for fifteen years took over the quarry lease. He lived at Whirlow Cottage with his wife, Ann, and their three children. Jonathan was born in Rowland in Derbyshire, and as a young married couple they appear to have moved around with his work as a quarryman, for his daughter, Emma, was born in Ashford, and his daughter, Matilda, in Stoney Middleton; John their son however was born in Ecclesall and in Whirlow the family put down their roots.

By 1881 Jonathan was employing five men. His son, John, had followed in his father's footsteps and in time he too took over the quarry which he ran in conjunction with the farm at Alms Hill, but by 1895 John appears to have become a full time farmer.

The land by the entrance to the Round Walk aside Fenney Lane still reveals the remains of quarry workings. Strata of rock show very clearly and on the 1854 Ordnance Survey map they are marked as old flagstone quarries.

WHINFELL

Tragically on 15th June 1971 Whinfell was gutted by fire. Situated near to Fenney Lane and bordering the old part of Ecclesall Road South at Whirlow Bridge, it was the home of two well known Sheffield families, first the Doncasters and then the Neills.

In 1897 Mr. Samuel Doncaster, the notable industrialist, commissioned the architect Norman Doncaster to draw up plans for a new house to be built on the quarry grounds at Whirlow Bridge. There were also plans for a three bedroomed lodge to be set thirty feet back from the Sheffield Hathersage Turnpike, but I don't think it was ever built. With no mains sewer the cesspool for the lodge had to be situated across the turnpike with the drain running under the road. Possibly for this reason it was decided to forego the lodge; in time Whinfell Cottages were built for the staff on land across the road from the main entrance.

In keeping with the other new homes in the area, the house was striking and imposing in appearance. It was approached from the main gates by a long carriage drive and these gates, although now blocked up, still remain fronting Ecclesall Road South; but houses now stand where the carriage drive used to be.

The house was to be provided with an internal water-closet on both the ground and first floors, a bathroom was to be installed on the first floor and two earth closets were to be built outside. There was a billiard room, drawing room, study, dining room and the usual kitchen offices and there were two staircases, the main one and a secondary one for the staff. In today's world, space is generally at a premium and houses are designed to make the most of every centimetre but when Whinfell was built there was space in abundance.

Whinfell, photographed for Sir Frederick Neill.

There were facilities for tools and fuel, a knife room, a further room to hold the engine and dynamo for making electricity; there was also space for a coach house and in 1898 plans were drawn up to build one. The coach house and stables were to be built away from the main house across the estate on land bordering the footpath that ran between Whinfell and Whirlow Grange; it was to be approached by a secondary drive off the main carriage drive. Built in stone with a paved yard for hard standing the coach house buildings included the stables, a harness room with hay loft above and a washing shed.

By 1902 the Doncaster family had moved into their handsome new home at Whinfell. Whin is another word for gorse, the yellow flowered shrub that grows on the hills around Whirlow. There were fields above Fenney Lane called the Whins. The gardens were very beautiful; in the spring there were the delights of the daffodils and rock garden and in the summer the luxuriant herbaceous borders.

Samuel Doncaster designed and planted the ornamental quarry garden in the old quarry. Rare shrubs and trees were brought to Whirlow to plant in these gardens and a series of rock pools were constructed with water flowing from one to the other. Bamboo and Japanese acers were grown to give form and autumn colour and flowering cherries, rhododendrons and stately conifers all added interest in this delightful garden.

The early part of the 20th Century was the time of some of the great plant hunters who worked with great diligence and often at great risk. Newly introduced trees, shrubs and flowers were arriving in England from all over the world and especially from the Far East. As we have seen in the other large houses in Whirlow, gardens had become all important, and their prosperous owners were able to indulge in this new found passion to display some of these new and exotic species in their own gardens. There was possibly an element

The Hall at Whinfell.

of competition too between these enthusiastic gentlemen who would be able to show and compare their latest acquisitions when neighbouring visitors came to call.

By 1933 Mr. Doncaster had moved to Whirlow Green, the home of his son-in-law and daughter, Dr. and Mrs. Charles Dyson Holdsworth, where he spent the rest of his days. He died aged 80 in 1934.

Whinfell passed to the Neill family. Federick Neill became the Master of the Company of Cutlers in Hallamshire in 1937 following in the footsteps of his father, James Neill, who had held the office in 1923. Prior to the Second World War, Osbert Skinner from the firm of family jewellers, took care of Mr. Neill's clocks. Every Thursday was clock winding day. Mr. Skinner would make his way up to Whinfell to carry out this duty. Good clocks with their delicate movements required careful handling. They also required someone with a strong grip to turn the large keys, a skill Mr. Skinner had developed with his years of experience. Mr. Neill, now Sir Frederick, remained at Whinfell until his death. In 1968 James Neill Holdings gave the Quarry Gardens to the City of Sheffield in memory of Sir Frederick Neill who had lived at Whinfell for thirty-one years.

The disastrous fire of June 1971 had so badly damaged the house that it was decided to sell the remainder of the estate. Whinfell was demolished in 1979 and in 1980 work began on building new houses, flats and bungalows; a new private road, Whinfell Court, replacing the main drive, was cut through from the old part of Ecclesall Road South.

WHIRLOW GREEN

In 1902 Alderman Clegg J.P. moved from Loxley House at Wadsley to Whirlow, where he had built a fine new home, Whirlow Green, on land adjacent to Whirlow Court which he leased from Earl Fitzwilliam. There were wonderful uninterrupted views across the fields and woods to Owler Bar.

William Clegg was a distinguished and successful lawyer who had joined the family firm of solicitors started by his father, William Johnson Clegg. As a young man he had defended the notorious Sheffield murderer, Charles Peace. A well known athlete, he was also actively involved in local and municipal affairs and became Lord Mayor of Sheffield in 1898/99; during the time he was living at Whirlow Green, he was knighted.

Whirlow Green, in its prime.

When Sir William left Whirlow Green the house was sold to Robert Greaves Blake, the son of Major William Greaves Blake of Mylnhurst, now the Convent School on Button Hill. The house was sold to John Middleton in 1920 and in 1927 to Dr. and Mrs. Charles Dyson Holdsworth. Mrs. Holdsworth, the daughter of Samuel Doncaster, the steel manufacturer, was returning to a part of Whirlow she knew well; her parents' home, Whinfell, was just across the main road from Whirlow Green.

In 1939 Herbert Hall purchased Whirlow Green. The Hall family lived there for the next twenty-one years before it was sold to Mr. and Mrs. J. Arthur Colver who were destined to be the last family to make it their home. The gardens at Whirlow Green were beautiful and the house was large and impressive. The Colvers remained there happily until 1985 when it was sold, the house and grounds being purchased by Ackroyd and Abbott, the builders. The house was pulled down in 1987 in preparation for new building in the future.

THE 20th CENTURY

For a time the imposing houses of Whirlow were to bring a new dimension to life in the area; they were peopled by men of power and influence, who were prepared to display their wealth and to entertain in the grand manner.

Many of the houses contained a billiard room, where the male members of the family and their friends could withdraw from female society to smoke their cigars and pipes and enjoy the game. The whole design of the room reflected the atmosphere of a gentleman's club, with polished mahogany, leather arm-chairs, sporting trophies and the elegant billiard table with the green baize top.

There were tennis parties on Saturday afternoons in summer, with tea on the lawn, a period of graciousness had arrived in Whirlow at least for certain strata of society.

The arrival of the Second World War and the changes in social life that followed, had a profound effect on the large Victorian house. They were built for sizeable families, with considerable numbers of domestic servants to run them, now a thing of the past; people needed smaller more easily run establishments and heating costs once minimal had become expensive. The vast gardens were impossible to look after without armies of gardeners; these once desirable residences had become anachronisms. When they came up for sale they were purchased not as family homes but for institutional or business purposes.

Some of the houses have been demolished: Whirlow House, Whirlow Green and Whinfell no longer remain. This area of Ecclesall Road South has been one of style and elegance. It is to be hoped that the planners of the future will retain this environment and not allow urban development to destroy its special character.

CHAPTER EIGHT

Postscript

THE changes that have evolved over the centuries in Whirlow from hamlet to outpost of a great estate, from wealthy residential area to desirable suburb have all left their mark. The fascination is that in so small an area life has been so varied and the occupations of its inhabitants so diverse. Today when Whirlow is mainly residential I hope you have found it interesting to look back to how men and women once lived and worked here.

Apart from the main occupations of farmer or small holder, Whirlow has had its corn mill and its quarries, its tan-yard and its scythe works. There have been besom makers, weavers, smelters, woodsmen, charcoal burners, cutlers, shoemakers, publicans, domestic servants, masons and joiners. And for the farmer's wife, whose life encompassed so many varied tasks, there was also puppy walking.

PUPPY WALKING

Joseph Hunter, in his book *Hallamshire,* records the great part hunting played in the life of the area we know of today as South Yorkshire. During the 18th Century not only the aristocracy but the cutlers too enjoyed participating in the sport; for the cutlers living in the villages, the countryside was on the doorstep. They were their own masters and could work and play to suit themselves. Consequently in the hunting season, Mondays and sometimes Tuesdays were the days chosen to go hunting. Unlike the Lords of the Manor and the landed gentry they hunted not on horseback but on foot; together with a pack of hounds they chased their quarry, the hare.

But there was fox hunting too and for the various Lords of the Manor and Masters of the hunt, there were hounds which required training. It is important to remember that in Whirlow in earlier times many of the farmers were tenants of the Lord of the Manor of Ecclesall and with their tenancies went duties, one of which was puppy-walking. Every year the farmers were sent a hound and they were to look after it and train it for a year. This was not always greeted with enthusiasm, it was another mouth to feed for which there was no pay. In fact in the 18th Century if they didn't carry out this duty, they were liable to be fined. In 1725 Elizabeth Allott of Little Common was told by the Ecclesall Manorial Court "we lay a pain (fine) also that unless Elizabeth Allott do within 14 days deliver up her dog to the Lord of the Manor or his gamekeeper, she shall forfeit £1.19s.11d". Elizabeth was not alone. Four farmers had been similarly warned in 1724!

The farmers of the 20th Century found it just as tiresome as their predecessors. It was usually left to the farmer's wife to take pity on the animal and to see that it didn't grow hungry. However reward did come at the end of the year when the hounds were taken down to the Waggon & Horses at Millhouses for the judging of the Top Dog. The dogs were collected from here and returned to Wentworth where judging took place and the farmer who produced the best hound was awarded a handsome cup. These cups are today prized possessions in the houses of the families whose forebears once won them.

RELIGION

Until now I have not mentioned the religions of the people in Whirlow. Booklets have already been written about the churches in Ecclesall and the part they played in the spiritual needs of the community; as part of the Parish of Ecclesall, Whirlow too shared in their history.

In the 17th Century many of the leading families in Sheffield were dissenters or nonconformists. William Stone, a joiner, who lived at Birley Field House, now Plumpton Cottages, was a dissenter, but I think the majority of the tenant farmers would find it easier and less troublesome to attend the established church at Ecclesall.

William appears to have been a man of some convictions, one prepared to take risks for the sake of his beliefs, for he was charged together with others

Plumpton Cottages 1969.

Plumpton House 1926. Formerly the home of William Tyzack, the founder of W. Tyzack, Scythe Manufacturers, of Abbeydale Works (Abbeydale Industrial Hamlet) and the Nicholson family.

with holding a nonconformist prayer meeting at Carbrook Hall, Attercliffe, quite some distance from Whirlow, in October 1684. He was living at Whirlow Mill in 1671 when his son Junia, is shown in the Cutlers' Company Records as becoming an apprentice cutler. According to Carolus Paulus he purchased Birley Field House from Thomas Lee of Thrift House in 1675, so he was obviously a man of comparative means.

William was employed by Sir John Bright, another notable dissenter, to work on the Whirlow Farms in 1679/80. As a joiner he would be a skilled craftsman, not only making furniture but one able to carry out specialised woodwork. In some of the Whirlow dwellings, he was required to lay the floorboards with seasoned wood and to make stairs and doors. What happened to him after his appearance at the quarter sessions held in Barnsley in October 1684? Sadly I do not know.

In 1861 Joshua Tyzack built Wood Lodge Chapel in the grounds of his house, Wood Lodge, on Abbey Lane. Joshua Tyzack was the son of William Tyzack the founder of W. Tyzack, the scythe manufacturers of Abbeydale Works; as a boy he had lived with his family at Plumpton House.

For a time the services at Wood Lodge Chapel were held in connection with Ecclesall Church, on Sunday and Tuesday evenings. The services on Sunday mornings and afternoons were taken by the preachers from the Methodist Reform Union; these services were often lively tub-thumping meetings, with

Ecclesall Church, circa 1850. The Pinfold for keeping stray animals was situated in front of the Church. Later it was moved to The Rising Sun, Abbey Lane.

the preacher sometimes banging the pulpit so hard that it made the lampshades quiver, thereby distracting the congregation from the message he was trying to deliver! Wood Lodge was demolished to make way for new development but Wood Lodge Chapel, now a house, remains.

During the 19th and early 20th Century, most of the families of the large houses in Ecclesall and Whirlow attended Ecclesall Church, their carriages waiting outside whilst they attended the service. The children were only too delighted if something untoward happened to lighten a rather tedious morning. For their strict Victorian parents, going to Church was not only an obligation to be fulfilled but also a social gathering and a way to meet the other families in the area.

Although seats were set aside for the "poor", many of the congregation would have pews which they rented for a small sum per annum, the money paying part of the Vicar's stipend. Sir John Statham purchased seats in Ecclesall Church from Henry and Dorothy Bright and the tenants of Whirlow Hall retained these pew rights at the church.

George Usherwood, writing *The Story of Ecclesall Church* in 1938, mentions the difficulties the Rev. T. Houghton experienced in 1908 when he decided to do away with this custom and make all the pews rent free. One can imagine the indignation this would engender from the wealthy patrons of the church, who would not like the change or the possibility of not obtaining a seat in their chosen position.

It was often customary for the wealthy citizens in the area to donate gifts to the church, sometimes in memory of a loved one. In 1849 a window was erected in the north transept of Ecclesall Church which contained the heraldic arms of Henry Furniss of Whirlow House. Possibly due to the many alterations that have taken place in the church, the window is no longer there, but the memorial tablet to Henry Furniss remains above the door in the south transept. In the early part of the 20th Century, services were held in the old school on Broad Elms Lane and in 1934 Earl Fitzwilliam gave some land at the corner of Whirlow Lane and Broad Elms Lane for the building of a church for the people of Whirlow. The anticipated population explosion in Whirlow did not happen and this church was not built, however when the Chapel of the Holy Spirit opened at Whirlow Grange Diocesan Conference Centre in 1958, it was for a time a daughter church of Ecclesall Church and services were held there regularly for the parishioners until 1973 when it returned to the Diocese.

THE MOTOR AGE

As we moved into the motorised age the pace of life increased in Whirlow as in other places. H. Keeble Hawson in *Sheffield: The Growth of a City* mentions a traffic census taken in September 1910 between the hours of 8.00 a.m. and 9.00 p.m. from Millhouses Lane to Whirlow Bridge. During those thirteen hours there were 279 horse drawn vehicles and surprisingly 120 motor cars, rather more than I should have imagined. Roadmen living at Parkhead cleaned the roads and removed the horse manure. But the days of the horse were

Parkhead. The Old Cottages with The Wheatsheaf on the right and a very narrow Ecclesall Road South, circa 1904. (The Sheffield Post Card Co.)

The Old Wheatsheaf, Parkhead. This old photograph was taken by Mr. Shipman who lived in the cottages across the road at Parkhead. The Blacksmith's Forge had become a garage to cater for the new automobile age.

nearly over, the smithy at the Wheatsheaf at Parkhead became a garage to cater for these new machines; people were becoming more mobile.

One of the greatest benefits for 20th Century Whirlow, must have been the abolition of the proposed plan to run the western outer ring road from Abbey Lane through Whirlow and across the hills to Fulwood. Fortunately the plan was abandoned. It would certainly have changed the face of Whirlow completely. In its wake more development would surely have followed and the attractive rural environs of Whirlow Hall Farm would have been lost for ever.

The needs of the city dweller for open spaces were beginning to be recognised; it was also realised that the old stone farms and cottages, so much a part of a past landscape, were part of our heritage and must not be destroyed. In 1981 the Final Green Belt Plan was approved by the City Council and after a Public Enquiry in 1982, Whirlow Hall Farm was included in the modified Green Belt Plan of 1983. For a time at least part of Whirlow is in the green belt; it is important for everyone that it remains so.

As we move towards the 21st Century, a modern and much larger Whirlow has emerged. But traces of the old remain, for as the traffic roars along the main highway at Whirlow Bridge, the old road, Fenney Lane, now virtually hidden, wends its way up the hill to Whirlow Hall Farm and the ancient seat of the Brights.

86

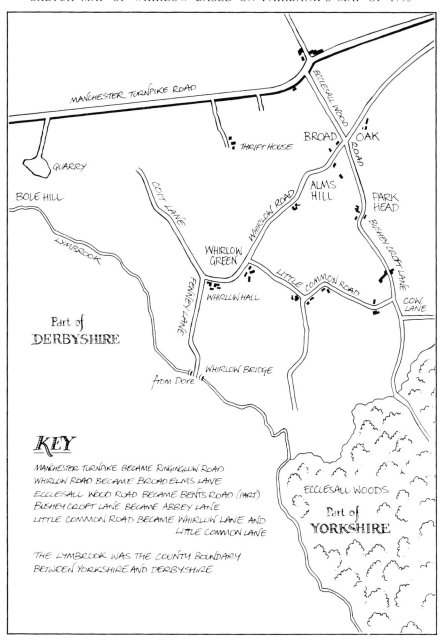

MANCHESTER TURNPIKE ROAD

ECCLESALL WOOD ROAD

THRIFT HOUSE

BROAD OAK ROAD

QUARRY

COIT LANE

ALMS HILL

WHIRLOW ROAD

PARK HEAD

BOLE HILL

BUSHEY CROFT LANE

LYMBROOK

WHIRLOW GREEN

FENNEY LANE

LITTLE COMMON ROAD

COW LANE

WHIRLOW HALL

Part of
DERBYSHIRE

WHIRLOW BRIDGE

from Dore

KEY

MANCHESTER TURNPIKE BECAME RINGINGLOW ROAD
WHIRLOW ROAD BECAME BROAD ELMS LANE
ECCLESALL WOOD ROAD BECAME BENTS ROAD (PART)
BUSHEY CROFT LANE BECAME ABBEY LANE
LITTLE COMMON ROAD BECAME WHIRLOW LANE AND
                         LITTLE COMMON LANE

THE LYMBROOK WAS THE COUNTY BOUNDARY
BETWEEN YORKSHIRE AND DERBYSHIRE

ECCLESALL WOODS

Part of
YORKSHIRE

SKETCH MAP SHOWING THE NEW TURNPIKE, THE WHIRLOW ROAD,
BASED ON THE ORDNANCE SURVEY MAP OF 1854.

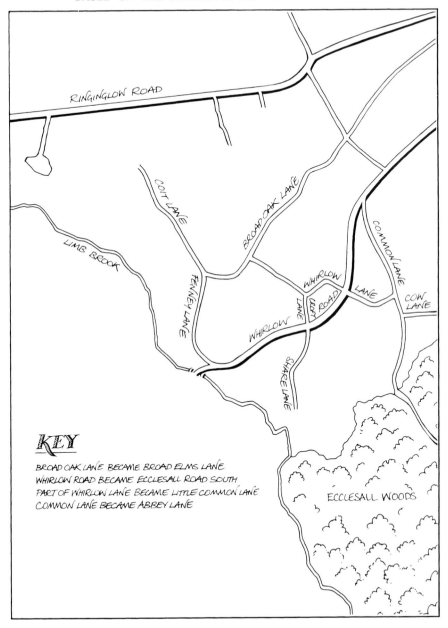

RINGINGLOW ROAD

COIT LANE

BROAD OAK LANE

LIMB BROOK

FENNEY LANE

COMMON LANE

WHIRLOW LANE

COW LANE

CROFT ROAD

WHIRLOW LANE

SHARE LANE

KEY

BROAD OAK LANE BECAME BROAD ELMS LANE
WHIRLOW ROAD BECAME ECCLESALL ROAD SOUTH
PART OF WHIRLOW LANE BECAME LITTLE COMMON LANE
COMMON LANE BECAME ABBEY LANE

ECCLESALL WOODS

Bibliography

Addy, S. O., *A Glossary of Words*. (1888).

Barley, M. W., *The English Farmhouse and Cottage*. (1961).

Bramhill, Mary M., *How They Lived in Old Ecclesall*. (1986).

Cobby, Rev. W., *A Walk Around Ecclesall*. (1873).

C.P.R.E., *The Story of Sheffield's Green Belt*. (1984).

Dodd, A. E. and E. M., *Peakland Roads and Tackways*, 1974.

Edwards, Brian, *Drawings of Historic Totley*. (1979).

Hall, T. W., *Descriptive Catalogue of the Jackson Collection*. (1914).

Hall, T. W., *Descriptive Catalogue of Early Charters in or Near Sheffield*. (1938).

Keeble Hawson, H., *The Growth of a City*. (1966).

Hey, David., *Buildings of Britain 1550-1750 Yorkshire*. (1981).

Hey, David., *The Rural Metal Workers of Sheffield*. (1972).

Hoskins, W. G., *The Making of the English Landscape*. (1955).

Hunter, Joseph., *Hallamshire (Gatty Edition)*. (1869).

Jackson, J. G., Johnson, G. F., Richmond, J. W., *The History of The Church of All Saints Ecclesall*. (1973).

Leader, R. E., *History of the Company of Cutlers in Hallamshire, Vol. 2*. (1906).

Meredith, Rosamund., *The Water Mills of Abbeydale*. (1974).

Miller, W. T., *The Water Mills of Sheffield*. (1936).

Oversby, Margaret., The section on the River Sheaf in *Water Power on the Sheffield Rivers*, Edited by David Crossley. (1989).

Paulus, Carolus., *The Manor and Parish of Ecclesall*. (1927).

Pike, W. T. & Addy, S. O., *Sheffield at the Opening of the 20th Century*. (1901).

Richardson, John., *The Local Historian's Encyclopedia*. (1974).

Leng, Sir W. C. & Co. (The Sheffield Telegraph) Ltd., *Sheffield and District Who's Who*. (1905).

Stainton, J. H., *The Making of Sheffield 1865-1914*. (1924).

Thomas, John., *Walks in the Neighbourhood of Sheffield*. (1830).

Transactions of the Hunter Archaeological Society, Vol. IV, Vol. X.

Usherwood, George Francis., *The Story of Ecclesall Parish Church*. (1938).

Vickers, J. Edward., *The Old and Historical Buildings of Sheffield*. (1968).

Walton, Mary., *A History of the Parish of Sharrow Sheffield*. (1968).

Young, Betty & Garland, Elizabeth (edited by), *From Dore to Dore*. (1973).

DIRECTORIES

Gales and Martin 1787. Reprinted by S. O. Addy. (1889).

Wardle and Bentham. Commercial Directory. (1814-1815).

William White. History and General Directory. (1833).

Kelly's Directories; Whites Directories.

DOCUMENTARY SOURCES

We are fortunate in Sheffield in having a wealth of archive and local studies material available for research, the primary sources in this book have been obtained from:

The Sheffield City Archives, this includes, The Wentworth Woodhouse Muniments; The Bagshawe Collection; The Bright Papers; Fairbank Collection of Maps, Enclosure Awards and Notebooks; the Hollis Collection; Jackson Collection; The Wheat Collection; Beauchief Muniments; Bush Sale Plans; Parish Records and Architectural Plans; John Gelley's Map and Field Book 1725.

The maps consulted include:
Bagshawe Collection, ref. C.301.
Fairbanks Collection, ref. S.3.L., S.4.L., S.8.L., M.B.455,, M.B.463., F.B.16,17.
Map of Sheffield 1795.
Hollis Collection, ref. L.D.1430, 1434, 1435R.
Wentworth Woodhouse Muniments, ref. W.W.M. Add Box 90, W.W.M. Add. Map.18.

THE LOCAL STUDIES DIVISION, SHEFFIELD CITY LIBRARIES

Census Returns 1841-1881.
Sale Plans and Maps.
Biographical Notes Mitchell-Withers by Stephen Welsh.
Local Pamphlets, Vol. 73, No. 17; Vol. 191, No. 5.
Collection of Newspaper Cuttings, Vol. 25; Vol. 27.
Drawings and Text from the unpublished work of Henry Tatton.

OTHER SOURCE MATERIAL HAS BEEN OBTAINED FROM:

The Borthwick Institute of Historical Research, York. Inventories and Wills.
Sheffield City Council Dept. of Planning and Design.
The Hollis Papers.
West Yorkshire Archive Service Wakefield, ref. Stone. QS1/23/10.
Ecclesall Church Parish Registers.

OTHER PRINTED MATERIAL

The Sheffield Spectator, Vol II. (Feb. 1972).
The Sheffield Telegraph. (21.2.62, 6.1.71, 9.11.71, 22.9.79).
The Star. (4.7.62, 27.4.89, 23.6.89)
Sheffield Weekly News. (4th February 1899).

Index

N.B. As the name Whirlow occurs so frequently it is not included in the index.
References to illustrations are in bold figures.

92

93

Sheffield City Libraries. Hollis Collection. LD 1430.

Sheffield City Libraries. Wentworth Woodhouse Muniments Add. Map 18 (part)